SAINT LAURENT

THE
PITCHFORK
REVIEW

OFFICIAL BALLOT
THE PITCHFORK REVIEW
ISSUE 11, FALL 2016

INSTRUCTIONS

1. Use BLACK PEN or PENCIL to fill in the oval.
2. To vote for a person whose name is printed on the ballot, fill in the oval ● to the right of the name of that person
3. To vote for a person whose name is not printed on the ballot, write or stick his or her name in the blank space provided and fill in the oval ● to the right of the write-in line
4. Do not vote for more candidates than the "VOTE for NOT MORE THAN #" for an office.
5. If you make a mistake, tear, or deface the ballot, return it to an election official and obtain another ballot.

DO NOT ERASE

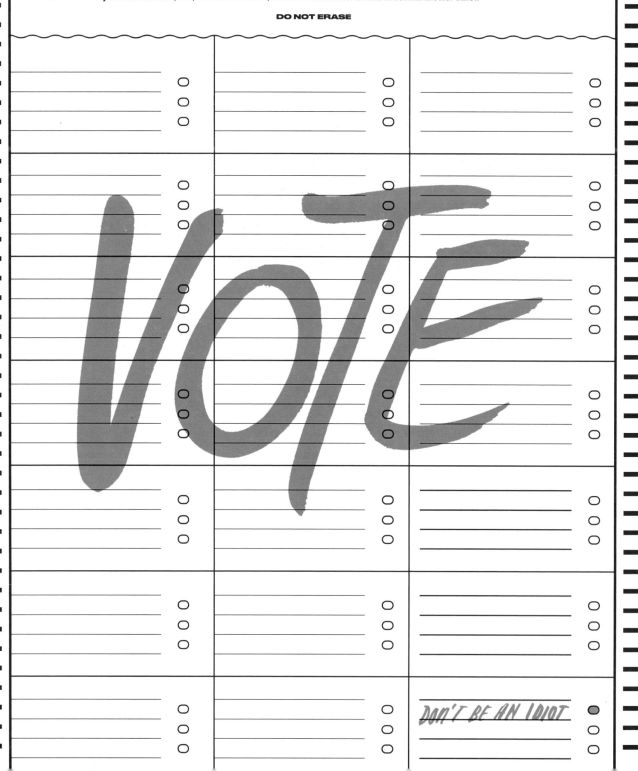

DON'T BE AN IDIOT

The Champagne of Beers

EVERY BUBBLE, A TINY AMBASSADOR OF QUALITY.

miller

HIGH LIFE

The Champagne of Beers

THE MUSIC POLITICS & ISSUE

CONTRIBUTORS

Adam Pally

Aleksandar Hemon

Alex Frank

Anders Holm

Andy Beta

Antony Huchette

Ariel Davis

Ava DuVernay

Camille Dodero

Carri Munden

Cleon Peterson

Courtney Duckworth

Denise Ho

DeRay Mckesson

Dischord Records

Dorian Lynskey

Esther Leung

Gaurab Thakali

Gerard Gaskin

James Brown

Jessica Viscius

Jillian Mapes

Joe Scarborough

Joy Reid

Kate Prior

Kathleen Hanna

Laura Callaghan

Llew Mejia

Mads Perch

Marc Hogan

Marc Masters

Mark Richardson

Matthew Schnipper

Melissa Etheridge

Michael Galinsky

Mike Renaud

Nadya Tolokonnikova

Ninni Nummela

Noelle Roth

Quinn Moreland

Rachael Finley

Rebecca Bengal

Ruth Pointer

Ryan Dombal

Sam Esmail

Sarah Mazzetti

Simon Reynolds

W. Kamau Bell

Wolfgang Tillmans

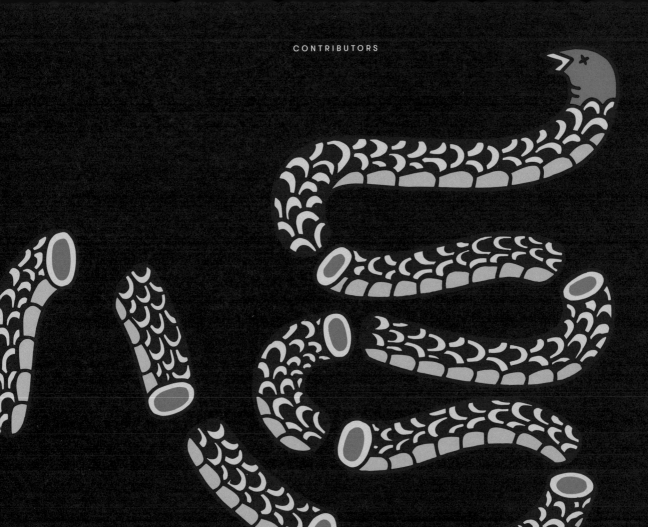

For the 11th issue of The Pitchfork Review, **SIMON REYNOLDS** wrote about the political influence of punk during his formative years: the Sex Pistols, Crass, The Style Council. Reynolds does see grime musicians and the duo Sleaford Mods as forces continuing the conversation started in the '70s. But he would hesitate to say that contemporary British musicians have the same political consciousness of the Sex Pistols or Crass. "A lot of people in Britain are very disillusioned with politics," says Reynolds, whose new book, *Shock and Awe: Glam Rock and Its Legacy*, comes out this fall. "Somewhere along the line, this idea that you could change things through music kind of broke down as a belief system." But instead of writing a song about what's wrong in the world, Reynolds believes that today's youth are more motivated to get directly involved with social change. "Perhaps you don't need songs, really. Perhaps the protests themselves, the movements, are enough."

—QUINN MORELAND

IN THIS ISSUE

TPR No. 11

THE
PITCHFORK
ISSUE
REVIEW

Ryan Schreiber
Editor-in-Chief/Founder
Chris Kaskie
President
Michael Renaud
Vice President &
Creative Director

Editorial
Mark Richardson
Executive Editor
Matthew Schnipper
Managing Editor
Amy Phillips
News Director
Becky Bass
Editorial Operations Director
Ryan Dombal
Senior Editor
Jayson Greene
Senior Editor
Jillian Mapes
Senior Editor
Jenn Pelly
Associate Editor
Evan Minsker
Associate Editor, News
Stacey Anderson
Associate Features Editor
Matthew Strauss
Associate Editor
Philip Sherburne
Contributing Editor
Marc Hogan
Senior Staff Writer
Kevin Lozano
Staff Writer
Noah Yoo
Staff Writer
Jazz Monroe
Associate Staff Writer
Sheldon Pearce
Associate Staff Writer

Quinn Moreland
Assistant Editor
Corey Smith-West
Editorial Fellow
Rachel Hahn
Editorial Fellow

Advertising
Zachary Davis
Head of Revenue
Matt Frampton
Vice President, Sales
Adam Krefman
Director, Sales &
Business Development
Brittany Oldham
West Coast Sales Director
Jared Heiman
Director, Sales
Seth Dodson
Integrated Marketing
Manager
Kara Tullman
Digital Campaign Manager
Lindsay Wold
Digital Sales Planner

Operations
John Jung
Vice President of
Strategy & Operations
Ryan Kennedy
Director of Finance
& Operations
Michael Chan
Social Media Manager
Bailey Constas
Associate Social
Media Manager
Courtney Cox
Business Operations
Associate
Amelia Dobmeyer
Internal Communications
Manager

Product
Matt Dennewitz
Vice President, Product
Neil Wargo
Senior Developer
Andrew Gaerig
Developer, Analyst
Alex Robertson
Developer

Design
Joy Burke
Digital Art Director
Noelle Roth
Art Director
Jessica Viscius
Senior Graphic Designer
Nicole Ginelli
Interactive Designer
Jojo Sounthone
Design Fellow

Video
RJ Bentler
Vice President,
Video Programming
Ash Slater
Producer
Michael Garber
Director
Jim Larson
Director
Jon Leone
Director
Rio Mineta
Editor
Anthony Esquivel
Motion Designer
Matt Caldamone
Motion Designer
Garrett Weinholtz
Channel Manager

This issue's editor was **MATTHEW SCHNIPPER**, who worked alongside **MARK RICHARDSON, CAMILLE DODERO, RYAN DOMBAL, JILLIAN MAPES,** and **QUINN MORELAND. COURTNEY DUCKWORTH** did the editing. It was designed and art directed by **NOELLE ROTH** and **JESSICA VISCIUS. RYAN KENNEDY, COURTNEY COX,** and **AMELIA DOBMEYER** looked after the operations.

The Pitchfork Review No. 10, Summer 2016 (ISBN 978-0-9975626-0-6) is published four times per year by Condé Nast, which is a division of Advance Magazine Publishers Inc. The Pitchfork Review Principal Office: 3317 W. Fullerton Ave., Chicago, IL 60647.

Condé Nast Principal Office: One World Trade Center, New York, NY 10007. S. I. Newhouse, Jr., Chairman Emeritus; Charles H. Townsend, Chairman;Robert A. Sauerberg, Jr., Chief Executive Officer and President; David E. Geithner, Chief Financial Officer; Jill Bright, Chief Administrative Officer.

Subscription rate in the U.S. for 4 issues is $49.99. Address all editorial, business, and production correspondence to Ryan Kennedy at ryank@pitchfork.com. Address all advertising inquiries to ads@pitchfork.com. For permissions and reprint requests, please contact info@thepitchforkreview.com. The Pitchfork Review is distributed by Publishers Group West and printed by Palmer Printing Inc., 739 S. Clark St., Chicago, IL 60605. Visit us online at thepitchforkreview.com. To subscribe to Condé Nast magazines on the World Wide Web, visit condenastdigital.com. Set in typefaces from Alias (alias.dj), Grilli Type (grillitype.com), and Klim Type Foundry (klim.co.nz). Printed on Mohawk Via and Endurance Cover Silk from Veritiv.

The Pitchfork Review does not read or accept unsolicited submissions and is not responsible for the return or loss of, or damage to unsolicited manuscripts, unsolicited artwork (including, but not limited to, drawings, photographs, and transparencies), or any other unsolicited materials.

Illustration by Michael Renaud.

INSTEAD OF A MORE TRADITIONAL SQUAD FLANKING HER, Beyoncé brought the mothers of Trayvon Martin, Eric Garner, Michael Brown, and Oscar Grant III as her guests to the red carpet for August's MTV Video Music Awards. Their presence was not announced beforehand, nor was it trumpeted by her in any onstage speeches. They simply stood, elegantly dressed like the celebrities they should not have had to be. Though Beyoncé, or any other artist, has no inherent responsibility to engage with social and political conversations through their work, **MUSIC HAS ALWAYS HAD SOMETHING TO SAY IN TIMES OF TROUBLE.** She and oters have been vocal in so many songs. In front of the cameras, outside of Madison Square Garden, these mothers' presence spoke strongly without having to actually say much.

Because, right now, what is there to say? Someone like the rapper YG has gone full throttle with his song "FDT (Fuck Donald Trump)." Subtlety seems like a luxury not afforded our current generation. "Your racist ass did too much." While YG may not be wrong, it seems unlikely this song, or any other, will be a unifier. But you take what you can get. With this issue of *The Pitchfork Review* we looked at times when songs have healed. Or at least tried to. Sam Cooke didn't lead the Civil Rights Movement, but his part is incalculably valuable. The Sex Pistols didn't prevent Margaret Thatcher's reign any better than the Nation of Ulysses got D.C. a voting representative in government (or founded a lawless new nation). But their music has been a salve and a spark.

THERE'S A LOT AT STAKE in America's election this November. Whatever happens, our nation is fractured, filled with anger and misinformation. It's dangerous for so many to simply walk outside. So much is up to our leaders to change. People, including many in this issue, are calling out to them. We can only hope **THEY WILL LISTEN.**

1

THE TRUTH IS IN

PHOTO BY MICHAEL OCHS ARCHIVES/GETTY IMAGES

THE MESS

Public Enemy's insoluble **FEAR OF**   BY DORIAN LYNSKEY
A BLACK PLANET *is problematic
because its world is problematic.*

FEAR OF A BLACK PLANET

was the first record I ever heard that seemed to contain far more information than I could possibly absorb. It was immediately obvious that Public Enemy leader Chuck D was trying to convey a hundred different things and that it would take the listener—or at least this listener—a long time to work out what they all were.

I was 16 and already interested in political music, but the other bands I liked felt safe and manageable. They were easy to co-sign because what they were saying made me feel like I was on the right side. At points on *Fear of a Black Planet*, I didn't even know where the right side was.

My confusion was partly that the 1990 album assimilates, and implicitly rebukes, the voices of Public Enemy's critics. Tracks like "911 Is a Joke" and "Burn Hollywood Burn" were self-contained and self-explanatory—they described the situations they were critiquing —but hearing "Contract on the World Live Jam" or "Incident at 66.6 FM" out of context felt like joining a TV series midway through season three, or hearing one side of an argument on the telephone. I knew that people were angry with Public Enemy, but who and why? I had no idea.

It was only later that I learned about the controversy that engulfed the group in the summer of 1989, after PE's then-minister of information Professor Griff was quoted making anti-Semitic remarks. (The ensuing outrage caused the Def Jam act to disband temporarily, then re-form soon after, with Griff repositioned as "supreme allied chief of community relations.") "Welcome to the Terrordome," the album's greatest and most complex track, was, I realized, an anxiously defiant communiqué from mediator Chuck D, a man who'd landed the task of defusing the media ruckus without jeopardizing band unity, and who had satisfied nobody—that he

SONGS

of change

To bring about social justice, history tells us, requires bold words and braver actions. Music, too, so often plays a role. The songs that help redirect a society's moral compass are sometimes explicit protest anthems; other times, they champion causes more surreptitiously, through sumptuous Philadelphia soul or hard-hitting hip-hop samples. TPR asked figures from the world of music and beyond—including visual art, literature, TV, film, and journalism— what political action songs they consider the most powerful.

Illustrations by
Antony Huchette

PUBLIC ENEMY, "FIGHT THE POWER"
W. Kamau Bell

Stand-up comic and host of CNN's
"United Shades of America"

This generation's "Fight the Power" might be Kendrick Lamar's "Alright," but to this day, "Fight the Power" doesn't sound dated. Maybe Chuck D's line, "Most of my heroes don't appear on no stamps" does, since Malcolm X has appeared on a [U.S. postal] stamp at this point, but the rest of the song just sounds like Public Enemy, in the same way that any track by Rage Against the Machine always sounds like Rage Against the Machine.

Also, I should add that I have Google alerts set for "Zack de la Rocha," so Zack de la Rocha's next song will probably be my new favorite protest song.

U2, "PRIDE (IN THE NAME OF LOVE)"
Ava DuVernay

Director of Selma, *and Netflix documentary* 13th, *screenwriter, producer (OWN drama "Queen Sugar")*

The first song that really resonated with me as a form of dissent was U2's "Pride (In the Name of Love)" when I was a really young teenager. I'm from Compton, so I wasn't really checking for, you know, white bands; in my neighborhood, people weren't rocking U2 very much. But someone told me that song was about Martin Luther King, Jr., so I listened to the words and was like, "This is dope." It talked about things that were important to me: I remember, early on, being very interested in issues of home-lessness, prison, presidents—there's a time as young people when you change from being of your family and you become of the world—and that was the soundtrack to those formative years. Eventually I got so, so into U2. They have been a huge influence on me. In fact, the last song from the "Queen Sugar" pilot ["Drowning Man," from 1983's *War*] was the first time I've ever had enough money to license a U2 song. My first film was called *I Will Follow*, which is a U2 song title, but I was so broke making that film [in 2010] I couldn't license the song, I only could name the film after it.

Protest music, when it's **REALLY INTERESTING** is a **MINEFIELD**

was saying, "Move as a team/Never move alone" at a moment when some members were barely communicating.

What I knew at the time, or what I could hear, was that Chuck was under immense pressure. On *It Takes a Nation of Millions to Hold Us Back*, Public Enemy's previous LP that I picked up soon afterward, he sounded superhumanly strong and wise. But on "Terrordome," he seemed backed into a corner, wildly swinging his fists at everyone who'd put him there. However hard he came at you, he had this tense, defensive quality. Not quite panic, but what precedes panic: a manic attempt to impose order on chaos. "Caught in the race against time, the pit and the pendulum." The unprecedented density of the Bomb Squad's organized bedlam added to the song's apocalyptic fever. And right in the middle of it were those explosive lines about "the Rab" and "the so-called chosen." Chuck always denied anti-Semitic intent, and his hot-tempered flailing was noth-ing like Griff's chillingly calm conspiracy theories, but his words caused further uproar and could never quite be explained away.

Encountering Public Enemy as a teenager left me with a lasting conviction that protest music, when it's really interesting, is a minefield. You can valorize anger and intellect but sometimes those qualities land artists in messes they can't escape. I couldn't disown PE and their peers even when they said things that were vexing—like the tossed-off homophobia of Black Planet's "Meet the G That Killed Me," or Ice Cube's horrific "Black Korea"—because those lyrics weren't aberrations.They came from the same place as their most fiercely righteous lines, which meant that you had to reckon with both if you wanted to understand either one. The history of political music—hell, any form of political engage-ment—tells us over and over that you can be radically progres-sive on one front and dismayingly reactionary on other; that your heroes can sometimes act like villains; that a sharp mind and a good heart have their limits.

That doesn't mean you give a free pass to anybody, if at all. Read contemporaneous coverage of Public Enemy and Ice Cube and you'll see conscientious critics wrestling hard with artists they find both magnificent and troubling. Call it hand-wringing if you like, but it's of a different order to the kind of knee-jerk moralizing that reduces critics to schoolteachers, choosing between approval and disapproval. Now more than ever, I distrust criticism which advances the idea that art is improved if you remove the problematic parts, like excising the poisonous organs from a pufferfish; *Fear of a Black Planet* is so heavy, overwhelming, and revealing *because* it's problematic—because the world it's describing is problematic. Dropping "Black Korea" from *Death Certificate* would be no sacrifice, but you can't cut out "Welcome to the Terrordome," *Fear of a Black Planet*'s maddened heart: "I got so much trouble on my mind.... "

In Philip Roth's 1998 novel *I Married a Communist*, one character says that an artist's job is "to impart the nuance, to elucidate the complication, to imply the contradiction. Not to erase the contradiction, not to deny the contradiction, but to see where, within the contradiction, lies the tormented human being. To allow for the chaos, to let it in. You must let it in." Some artists do that consciously, but others reveal the contradiction despite themselves. Chuck's intention in "Welcome to the Terrordome" is to draw a line under a controversy and get everyone off his back, but his frantic, overheated delivery, verging on stream-of-consciousness, betrays his confusion—and the palpable instability it creates is more compelling than his explicit agenda. Like the Sex Pistols' "Bodies," or the Manic Street Preachers' "Of Walking Abortion," or Sly and the Family Stone's "There's a Riot Goin' On," or a 1970s Nina Simone concert, the song leaves the listener no safe place to stand because the artist has no safe place to stand. To hear that instability from Chuck D, whose standard mode is iron-clad certainty, is thrilling and unnerving. What if he's as confused and fallible as anybody?

No matter how much I've learned about the circumstances surrounding *Fear of a Black Planet* since it first ambushed me in 1990, it still feels insoluble. It's an hour-long argument with everybody; deciding whether or not to endorse or to excuse every detail is fruitless. You just have to plunge into the mess because the truth is in the mess—the truth that separates art from propaganda. Intentionally or otherwise, *Fear of a Black Planet* lets in the chaos. ✍

DORIAN LYNSKEY *is the UK-based author of* 33 Revolutions Per Minute: A History of Protest Songs.

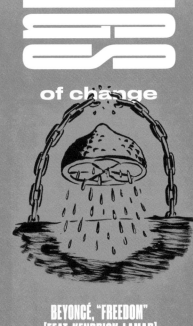

of change

BEYONCÉ, "FREEDOM" [FEAT. KENDRICK LAMAR]
DeRay Mckesson
Black Lives Matter activist

"Freedom" is a hymnal—an ode to blackness, to protest, and to liberation. Beyoncé and Kendrick deftly highlight police violence, the central role black women have always had in freedom work, and the black community's strength to survive and to thrive despite the odds.

Read our interview with Mckesson on page 114

BOYSETSFIRE, "AFTER THE EULOGY"
Rachael Finley aka "Steak" Anderson
Fashion designer, Instagram star, host of MTV's "Wonderland"

Seeing this band live is what got me into hardcore music. This song is raw emotion with "No justice/No peace" chanted in the background, gang-vocal style. Lyrically, it touches on other issues, like immigration and refugees: "How many dying millions/ Have to crawl to our front doorsteps?" At first, I was hyped because this was such an easy pick—it's an older song that's still relevant to what's going on right now. But when you actually think about it, that's super disgusting. What does that say for our progress?

PROTEST SOUL

On the **UNRELENTING POWER** of Sam Cooke's essential civil rights anthem, "A Change Is Gonna Come." BY REBECCA BENGAL

In the last few years, you hear it everywhere. After Trayvon Martin, Mike Brown, Eric Garner, Tamir Rice, Sandra Bland, Freddie Gray; after the mass shooting at Emanuel A.M.E. Church in Charleston and the Pulse nightclub massacre in Orlando; after those deaths, and so many others, marchers and mourners have sang it—out in the streets, at candlelight vigils, and at protests—distinctly echoing the civil rights demonstrations of the 1960s. Sam Cooke's "A Change Is Gonna Come" has been covered, over the years, in melting, slow-burning, and rousing versions by Otis Redding, Aretha Franklin, Tina Turner, Luther Vandross, R. Kelly, the Supremes, Solomon Burke.

I have a personal weakness for Baby Huey's aching rendition, with its scorching shriek and ad-libbed, psychedelic refrain. Lately, we've come to know the protest anthem in sorrow and solidarity, but two elections ago, when soul singer Bettye LaVette performed the standard on the Lincoln Memorial steps, her performance transmitted a sense of joy and hope: In two days, America would inaugurate the first black man as President. You could even excuse the oddness of the choice to make Jon Bon Jovi her duet partner because of the sheer sense of joy and hope that he, too, radiated about the moment.

Forty-four years earlier, Cooke sang "A Change Is Gonna Come" on "The Tonight Show Starring Johnny Carson." It would be the first and only time he'd perform it and the tape of that night has been lost. The arrangement was too complex—they'd had to scramble to get musicians together for the Carson spot—and the song, which had come to him almost whole and vision-like, spooked him. He worried that the stanza he'd written about Jim Crow laws ("I go to the movies/And I go downtown/Somebody keep tellin' me/Don't hang around")

would be too controversial. Those lines were cut for radio play when the single, released as the B-side to the Top 10 hit "Shake," came out in December 1964.

The events that inspired "Change," and specifically those lyrics, occurred one night the previous fall. The date was Oct. 8, 1963, nearly a century after the 13th Amendment abolished slavery; 10 years after the Brown v. Board of Education decision desegregated public schools; nine years after Emmett Till's murder in Mississippi; seven years and 10 months after Rosa Parks refused to give up her bus seat in Montgomery; and four years after the Woolworth lunch counter sit-ins in North Carolina. But it was also only four months after activist Medgar Evers' assassination, two months after the March on Washington, and three weeks after the 16th Street Baptist Church bombing in Birmingham. The Civil Rights Act of 1964 wouldn't be passed for another six months.

So that October night, Cooke, his wife Barbara, and his entourage headed to a Holiday Inn in Shreveport, La., where they'd called ahead to reserve rooms. By this point, Mississippi-born

19

crooner was a recognizable rock'n'roll star with more than a dozen Top 40 hits on the Billboard Hot 100; he'd performed on national television programs like "The Ed Sullivan Show" and "The Dick Clark Show." Yet when the 32-year-old pulled into the motel driving in a $60,000 Maserati, his band riding in a Cadillac limousine, the sharply dressed group of black guests were told that suddenly, inexplicably, there was no availability. A commotion ensued, with Cooke reportedly arguing with the hotel manager and the caravan's limo honking boisterously outside in retaliation. The cops were called, the incident of the "negro band leader" trying to register at a "white motel" made the *New York Times*, and Cooke, charged with disturbing the peace, spent the night in jail.

Creatively, Cooke had been heading toward "Change" for months. Earlier in 1963, he heard a song he wished he'd written—or at any rate, one he believed a black man should sing: Bob Dylan's "Blowin' in the Wind," which he almost immediately incorporated into his live repertoire. In Cooke's hands, Dylan's plaintive folk became uptempo—downright peppy, even. No wonder, really, he connected with the song: The melody was borrowed from "No More Auction Block For Me," a spiritual that first gained renown as a marching song for black Civil War soldiers and also shaped the greatest marching hymn of them all, "We Shall Overcome." But Dylan's mimicry wasn't so much theft as an intentional reference, a clear signal of the song's self-awareness, and an homage to the greater historical tradition the acoustic anthem was meant to honor. As Dylan told a journalist about "Auction Block" in 1978, "'Blowin' in the Wind' sorta follows the same *feeling.*"

"Change" became essential to that lineage. Driven by the injustice of that night in Shreveport, the song had come to him almost whole and vision-like. The opening movement's strings stirred with thunderous suspense and

then in an exhalation, the singer's entire life pours out: "I was born by the river in a little tent," Cooke sings, "Ohh and just like the river I've been running ev'r since." There is a golden weariness in that voice: heavy, pleading, resilient, still believing. It's the sound of a solitary wanderer: He is mythic, he is epic, he is Everyman, he is Moses, he is the Invisible Man, but he is alone. "It would just go all through your bones," said Mavis Staples, whose father would later write a kindred gospel number "Why (Am I Treated So Bad)" about the Little Rock Nine. You could call this movement *protest soul.*

It's impossible to hear "Change" now and not feel a whisper of the omens Cooke likely felt—change tinged with foreboding. I listened to it again one Sunday evening late this summer. The streets had baked all day in a humid, oppressive heat, and my neighborhood in Brooklyn felt oddly soundless and empty. The wall outside Spike Lee's 40 Acres and a Mule film company headquarters, which has become a de facto neighborhood memorial, had just added two new posters, commemorating the abruptly ended lives of Alton Sterling in Baton Rouge, La. and Philando Castile in Falcon Heights, Minn. Days before, the activist Reverend William Barber II, organizer of civic protests in my own embattled home state of North Carolina, had taken the stage at the Democratic National Convention. "We must listen to the ancient chorus," he exhorted the country in florid, an almost musical phrasing. "It is possible to shock a bad heart. We are called upon to be the moral *defibrillators* of our times." When I came home and put on Cooke's record as I'd done so many other times recently, I let the sweeping lonely dream of it fill the room.

The spirit of familiarity that haunts protest soul, from "Auction Block" down to "Change," is intentional, the handed-down quality of traditional music, an extended conversation with the ancient chorus. The power of "Change" thrives on these deep roots, its lonesome singer sustained by that river. If Dylan issued a call, posed the question—"Yes, and how many years must some people exist/Before they're allowed to be free?"—"Change" was Cooke's answer. He was that wind, restless, still delivering. The song's apex, half a century later, deals a devastating blow: "Then I go to my brother/And I say brother help me please/But he winds up knockin' me/Back down on my knees."

The complete version of the song, lyrics intact, finally appeared on *Shake*, Cooke's posthumous album released January 1965, a month after he died of a gunshot wound in a Los Angeles motel. "It's been too hard living/But I'm afraid to die/'Cause I don't know what's up there/Beyond the sky," he sang. And "Change" represents his greatest achievement, his last words in a final bid that resonates so deeply today: "It's been a long, a long time coming/But I know a change is gonna come, oh yes it will." ✍

ELVIS COSTELLO & THE ATTRACTIONS, "(WHAT'S SO FUNNY 'BOUT) PEACE, LOVE, AND UNDERSTANDING"
Joe Scarborough

Host of MSNBC's "Morning Joe," Morning Joe Music frontman

As a guy who's looking at my party and wondering what the hell is happening to it, I vote for Elvis Costello's "(What's So Funny 'Bout) Peace, Love, and Understanding." You look at the ugliness of the Republican primary, you look through the polls, and you see that a large number of Americans actually support a ban on Muslims entering the United States. And you wonder how many of those people have any understanding about what the First Amendment means, who it's supposed to protect, and why our Founders actually came to this country—which was to escape religious persecution. Now we have a campaign that has succeeded by separating the majority from the quote-unquote others—whether the others are Mexicans, Muslims, Syrians, or people who want to immigrate to this country—but except for Native Americans, we're a nation of immigrants. That's why Elvis Costello's anthem off of [1979's] *Armed Forces* is right for the time. I'd love to hear a party play it as the candidates walked off the stage.

BIKINI KILL, "REBEL GIRL"
Nadya Tolokonnikova

Activist and member of Russian feminist punk rock protest group Pussy Riot

This song made my life and now it's making the life of my daughter, who's eight years old and listening to Bikini Kill. She loves this song. That's my way to teach her about feminism: Every time she wants to cry, I just turn on this song, and it works like magic.

3

BY
MARC
HOGAN

In 2004, a scrappy EP of political punk covers aimed to remind fans the year's presidential election wasn't a choice, but an ULTIMATUM. Three inaugurations later, Poster Children's *On the Offensive* is a reminder of how much innocence we've LOST—and how much every little bit matters.

THE LAST EXIT

Poster Children have lived up to their name. Formed in 1987 from the ashes of a group that covered Joy Division and Butthole Surfers, the Champaign, Ill., quartet was, in many ways, an archetypal indie rock band of the time. They used punk's vitality and power-pop's sense of melody. They toured relentlessly and took a do-it-yourself approach to tasks like artwork and merch design. They recorded with Steve Albini and joined a major label during that crazed post-Nirvana moment when majors were signing everybody. And then, at the end of the 1990s, Poster Children returned to independent life.

In those first 13 years, Poster Children released seven albums and an EP, plus another two LPs under their ambient-instrumental alias, Salaryman. They took a breather in the early 2000s, when cofounders Rick Valentin and Rose Marshack had a child. The band resurfaced in January 2004, with an eighth album, *No More Songs About Sleep and Fire*, that brought previous political undertones explicitly to the foreground ("The leader represents the one percent who pay his rent," Valentin declares on "The Leader"). Then, in September 2004, Poster Children put out one more release: an EP called *On the Offensive*, consisting of six politically themed cover songs, pegged to President George W. Bush's bid for reelection against then-Senator John Kerry.

At the time, I was 22, and despite college years spent constantly downloading music, I was still pretty freshly acquainted with the group. I was also intensely focused on that year's presidential election—a kind of referendum, in my view, on an incumbent who misled a grieving nation into a disastrous war, dismantled environmental

23

ELTON JOHN, "PHILADELPHIA FREEDOM"
Kathleen Hanna

*Activist, singer for the Julie Ruin and
Le Tigre, co-founder of Bikini Kill*

"Philadelphia Freedom" is on every mixtape I make. It was written [in 1975] because Elton wanted to write something for his best friend, Billie Jean King, who basically invented women's tennis in the United States. She was my hero as a kid; I have a photograph in my office of Billie Jean King and Arthur Ashe dancing at a party. When she first came on the scene, women's tennis was smaller than the WNBA—it was like women's slow-pitch softball. Women were not given the same amount of prize money [as men] and she demanded [more] money. She also started a women's tennis organization, got sponsors, and that was a big deal. It was like: "You're selling feminism out"; "You're selling gay rights out, because you're [working] with Virginia Slims cigarettes." There's been a lot of talk lately about how if capitalism even touches feminism, it's somehow tawdry and not real anymore, but I always love to think back to her making that compromise. Now, women's tennis is an amazing sport in which women hold almost an equal footing to men—and a lot of that is King's contribution. Sometimes we have to negotiate within the capitalistic world we live in to make change, and there's no shame in that.

But the real thing for me is that "Philadelphia Freedom" is a love song between a gay man and a lesbian. That's so big culturally. When I hear it, I always feel joyous and think of Billie Jean King and Elton John hanging out.

protections, fought with particular cynicism against gay marriage, and lavished tax cuts on the wealthy while wrecking the economy. In other words, this was an election that mattered. While getting paid through a temp agency to edit AOL's soon-to-be-defunct city guides hadn't exactly allowed me to start up my own 527 lobbying fund, writing an obscure progressive political blog, with a friend and co-worker, felt like a small way of making our voices heard in the electoral process. In fact, it was a pen pal from the liberal blogosphere who introduced me to Poster Children in the first place.

Coming a year after the U.S.-led invasion of Iraq, 2004 saw no shortage of political music. The same day Poster Children unveiled *On the Offensive*, Green Day issued their much-ballyhooed "punk rock opera" *American Idiot*. Everyone from Bruce Springsteen, R.E.M., and Dixie Chicks to Bright Eyes, Death Cab for Cutie, and My Morning Jacket hit the road that year with MoveOn's Vote for Change tour. Steve Earle dropped an LP proclaiming, *The Revolution Starts Now*. Fat Mike of NOFX put together two *Rock Against Bush* compilations, featuring big names like Foo Fighters and No Doubt.

On the Offensive was different. It wasn't a grandiose concept album auditioning for a short run on Broadway. There was no instantly dated subject matter, like Earle's song devoted to "American Taliban" John Walker Lindh. Valentin and Marshack co-hosted a progressive radio show on Poster Children's website, but they weren't famous people. *On the Offensive* channeled the band's righteous fury through music that had already proved it could last—but instead of the usual Vietnam War-era relics, these were songs born out of punk: the Clash's *London Calling* capitalism critique "Clampdown," Heaven 17's BBC-banned Reagan diss "(We Don't Need This) Fascist Groove Thang," X's disillusioned Election Day anthem "The New World" (with its heartbreaking mantra "Don't forget the Motor City"), Fear's jingoism-eviscerating "Let's Have a War," Hüsker Dü's paranoid guitar-riff clinic "Divide and Conquer," and XTC's Left-vs.-Right brooder "Complicated Game." All were songs I wanted to know better, all seemed to apply to the Bush administration, and Poster Children played their mostly faithful renditions with sweaty, hard-hitting urgency. "What are we gonna do now?" Valentin and

Marshak began the EP in half-shouted harmony. The answer was in their music: *This*. Something. Whatever they could.

The punk ethos and progressive ideology of *On the Offensive* were related. Poster Children arose out of an epiphany that bands didn't have to sound ready for corporate rock radio. "You could make up for technical talent with energy and directness," Valentin told the *New York Times*' Jon Pareles in 1991. "It was the realization that, 'Hey, I can do this.'" When I had my own opportunity to interview Valentin, ahead of an October 2004 gig in Chicago, he cast his EP's political goals in a similarly participatory light. "There has to be a groundswell of voices rising up against the current administration; it's so much easier to voice your opinion and exercise your rights when you see someone else doing it," he emailed. "We want this EP to be one of the many little angels standing on the shoulders of potential voters, telling them to participate and make a difference, fighting off the noise from the mass of little devils whispering that they have no voice in our society and have no reason to vote." Valentin had been a strong supporter of third-party candidates, objecting to the idea of picking "the lesser of two evils," but this year he didn't think he had that luxury. "I feel like we're approaching the last exit."

No one then could have known how much innocence we still had left to lose. To many, the 2016 election feels like an even more final choice, perhaps an apocalyptic one, between a pathologically bullying, Putin-embracing, undisguised-racist troll and a deeply unpopular, yet thoroughly experienced, mainstream political tactician. Online, the decentralized world of individuals finding each other through blogrolls has long since given way to the top-down proclamations of celebrities and brands on social media, which has turned into an echo chamber where you could pretty much exist seeing only opinions and biases you share, or interests you already have, indefinitely. Even rock's response to the general election has been mostly limited to a political EP from a super-group of Rage Against the Machine, Public Enemy, and Cypress Hill members, which stinks. But *On the Offensive* sticks with me. And now—when it really feels like we're approaching the last exit— it inspires me. There has to be a groundswell of voices rising up against Trump's for-real fascist groove thing; it's so much easier to voice your opinion and exercise your rights when you see someone else doing it. "Don't forget the Motor City/This was supposed to be the new world." *What are we gonna do now?*

Poster Children, for their part, are touring again this fall. What are the rest of us gonna do now? Hopefully, remember that change still begins with the realization that, "Hey, I can do this"—and then, whatever little bit we can, while we still can. ✎

of change

AUDRA DAY, "RISE UP"
Joy Reid

*MSNBC political analyst
and host of "AM Joy"*

The current song I play is "Rise Up" by Audra Day. The lyrics are beautiful. When I found out that she would be at the [2016] Democratic National Convention, I was very excited, because I hadn't heard her sing live. The moment she performed it, right after the Mothers of the Movement [a nine-woman group whose African-American children have been killed by police or died from gun violence], was so incredibly moving and inspirational, it doubled my appreciation for the song.

We are living through a time that is particularly dark. We have a candidate on the Republican side who's not just unusual, but kind of frightening. You have a lot of people following him in part because they're afraid of change or what the country is becoming. Then, on the other side, you have people who are terrified of that spectacle actually becoming our presidency, our standard-bearer. In this frightening time, this song just gives me hope.

CHER, "WOMAN'S WORLD"
Ruth Pointer

Founding member of the Pointer Sisters

A couple of weeks ago, I was in my car and this [2013] song Cher recorded came on—and it drove me crazy: I don't know who you're supporting, but I'm With Her. I thought, "Girl, you need to be pumping this song on every station right now."

Also, I love the Fleetwood Mac song Bill Clinton used, "Don't Stop": "Tomorrow will soon be here" is *right*.

PHONES DRONES AND COUNTRY MUSIC

Sturgill Simpson's rollicking rager "Call to Arms" takes aim at our WORST ENEMY— ourselves. BY JILLIAN MAPES

Where I grew up in northeast Ohio was so blue-collar, Bruce Springsteen used its shuttered steel mills to illustrate America's crumbled Rust Belt in *The Ghost of Tom Joad*'s "Youngstown." But despite this working-class mentality, which typically makes the area lean blue in presidential elections, it is not exactly a liberal place. In high school, as identities began to gel, the boys in my honors classes emerged as wannabe rednecks with George W. Bush bumper sticks on their Chevys. They seemed to pride themselves on being "fiscally responsible," but I couldn't resist arguing with stubborn male peers adopting close-minded logic—that was how those friendships worked. In the years following 9/11, as America flooded the Middle East with soldiers not much older than me, I spent a lot of time driving around the Midwest in pickup trucks listening to Kenny Chesney. It was on these drives that I tried to explain the virtues of John Kerry and Radiohead's *Hail to the Thief* (the ultimate anti-Bush record); my conservative pals countered with the merits of Karl Rove and Toby Keith. Ultimately, I chalked it up as a failed thought experiment, with one measurable result: I will know the words to Keith's "I Love This Bar" until the day my body leaves this earth.

After that, I avoided country music for a long time. The turning point was probably the 2013 release of Kacey Musgraves' "Follow Your Arrow," a do-what-you-want declaration inclusive of gay folks and stoners and straight-up weirdos. But it was Sturgill Simpson's 2014 LP *Metamodern Sounds in Country Music* that really brought me back into the fold. This album is pure cosmic trash, and I couldn't love it more. "Don't have to do a goddamn thing 'cept sit around and wait to die," Simpson boasts on the indelible single "Living the Dream." But by this spring's *A Sailor's Guide to Earth*, Kentucky's finest singer-songwriter claimed to know a thing or two about how to live. The record is written from the point of view of a sailor unsure if he'll come back alive, in the form of a letter to his wife and young son back home. With this concept in mind, Simpson brings something entirely new to a song as ubiquitous as Nirvana's "In Bloom": Where Cobain sang about lamestreamer fans who couldn't understand his band's gravity, Simpson seems to have a more literal take on the chorus couplet: "And he likes to shoot his gun/But he don't know what it means."

Simpson served a couple of years in the Navy right out of high school, and though he never ended up on the frontlines, the experience certainly seems to color his view of the military. Nowhere is this made clearer than on *A Sailor's Guide to Earth*'s five-and-a-half-minute closer, "Call to Arms," where Simpson takes the lingering effects of the War on Terror, compounds them with media noise and the digital age's narcissism, and sets the whole shebang ablaze with a distinctly punk-rock anti-establishment rage.

Millennials have been (rightly) dubbed the "me me me" generation, but what Simpson underscores is that all that "me" can manifest into dangerous ignorance regarding matters that don't seem to directly affect us, since they don't play out on our timelines. The following verse is very likely the best thing Simpson has ever written, and may ever write:

Nobody's looking up to care about a drone / All too busy looking down at our phone / Our ego's begging for food like a dog from our feed / Refreshing obsessively until our eyes start to bleed / They serve up distractions and we eat them with fries / Until the bombs fall out of our fucking skies

And yet "Call to Arms" often overflows with pure and unstoppable musical joy. Simpson channels his jaded disgust into a rollicking rager and staffs the shindig's band with Stax-loving horn players (i.e. the Dap-Kings) and honky-tonk pianists who eventually crescendo out of control. By the end, the burgeoning maverick surmises—with a festering rancor rarely heard on major-label country albums anymore—"Bullshit's got to go." He burns down everything in pursuit of the "truth," with an urgency as if this is life or death. Because it is.

The first time I heard "Call to Arms" back in March, it felt exactly like what Simpson's weighty title promised. Five years since we officially withdrew troops from Iraq, our military presence there continues to creep upwards—toward nearly 5,000 troops, as of this spring—in an effort to take back Mosul from ISIL. It was right around this number of troops who lost their lives in Iraq the first time, at the hands of a war about pride and oil that large swaths of the population chose to ignore long before it even ended. I couldn't be one of those people anymore—someone who tunes out bad news because narcissistic frivolity is more fun. This is what great protest music does—it wakes you. I remembered who I was at 16 when I'd argue with faux-hillbilly boys about what America should and shouldn't be. When I went home this fall, I rode around town feeling depressed about all the Trump signs I saw and blasted "Call to Arms" the entire time. I half-hoped I'd run into the old gang. I was ready for a fight. ✑

of change

THE CLASH, "SPANISH BOMBS"
Aleksandar Hemon

Bosnian-born author of novels
Nowhere Man *and* The Lazarus Project

I'm old enough to remember when *London Calling* came out [in 1979]. When I was growing up [in communist Yugoslavia], we couldn't go to the store and buy it. Someone's father or mother brought it from London and then we shared the album. "Spanish Bombs" is a great song, but as a kid, I was a history buff, so to have a song by a punk band about the Spanish Civil War was a revelation.

ENNIO MORRICONE & JOAN BAEZ "HERE'S TO YOU"
Wolfgang Tillmans

German fine-art photographer and Frank Ocean collaborator

I've loved Joan Baez since I was a teenager. This deep sense of compassion, peace, and understanding that emanates from her voice, I just can't resist. I found the [1971] song again a few years ago and was blown away by its simplicity. Then I read up about the Sacco and Vanzetti affair, which it is about: a miscarriage of justice that resulted in a death penalty. The death penalty is one thing about the United States I find difficult to understand—it's so abhorrent. To dedicate a song to that is incredibly powerful, and there's something in her voice that's so encouraging. It's not just anger or protest, it's an energy that encourages you to speak out.

of change

JAY Z, "99 PROBLEMS"
Adam Pally

Actor and comedian (ABC's "Happy Endings," FOX's "The Mindy Project")

This is hard to justify as a protest song, but "99 Problems." The second verse where Jay goes in and out of the cop voice, talking to himself getting pulled over—we're talking, what, 12 years ago? "'Son, do you know why I'm stopping you for?'/'Cause I'm young and I'm black and my hat's real low?'" Every white kid knows every word to that song. I bet every cop knows every word to that song. But now, that song is so fucking important. Especially that verse.

PETER GABRIEL, "BIKO"
Melissa Etheridge

Activist, singer-songwriter, cannabis entrepreneur

This song is always on the top of my list. It's the beat, how Peter Gabriel paints a picture of [anti-apartheid activist] Stephen Biko in his cell, and in the end we all want to sing together. This took place after the American Civil Rights Movement, in Africa: To see the atrocities still happening there and understanding that, even though the situation was thousands of miles away, it still affected us—that was important.

The Backwoods Barbie's riches-in-rags fable **"COAT OF MANY COLORS"** may be 45 years old, but in 2016, it's just the song America **NEEDS.**   BY ALEX FRANK

OLLY
FOR

EVERYONE

WHEN DOLLY PARTON WAS A CHILD, her mother looked at a box of tattered old rags and saw a Technicolor dream coat. So goes the 1971 classic "Coat of Many Colors," on which Dolly sings about how her mom once transformed left-behind scraps of fabric into a one-of-a-kind garment, telling her young daughter the biblical story of Joseph as she worked. Dolly grew up without electricity and running water, sharing beds with her 11 brothers and sisters in a small house in the Smoky Mountains of Tennessee, but she remembers feeling rich anyway because she had a house full of love.

As the song's lyrics go, she was proud to put the coat on once it was finished, and though the other kids at school made fun of her for having threadbare clothing, it didn't bother her a bit. "My coat of many colors was worth more than all their clothes," Dolly sings. "One is only poor only if they choose to be."

"Coat of Many Colors" is a lovely fable, a rosy way to mythologize a childhood that was likely filled with its share of challenges. Dolly has long said that it is her most personal song—no small thing considering that the 70-year-old has penned more than 3,000. "To me, it's more than a song," she told an interviewer last year. "It's an attitude. It's a philosophy." And, in 2016, I've come to see it as something even bigger: a comforting, critical ethos worth heeding in a troubling age. In this year of shootings and endless struggles, with an election cycle that has elevated all our anxieties instead of soothing them, the sage wisdom of a song like "Coat of Many Colors" reminds us of something essential about the American can-do spirit. And, in a broader sense, at a moment when the idea of basic national identity feels like it is ripping apart at the seams—when class and geography and race are built up to be insurmountable barriers—Dolly offers us a little respite from this insanity and, perhaps, a way forward.

Dolly is a rural white person from the center of the South who has found just as much of a home in the hearts of fans in big cities on the coasts. She never lost the rugged

DOLLY
is **PROOF** *there's still something* **GOOD**
in this fractured **NATION.**

charm that makes her a country girl, all while finding ways to build roads between communities that, from some vantage points, seem further apart than ever. "Been a lot of Bible Belt folks that don't accept a lot of things and a lot of people. But I just always had a very open mind and a very open heart," she told the A.V. Club in 2011 when asked about her relationship with her adoring LGBT fans. "I appreciate getting accepted myself, because I know I'm unusual. And I love the unusual in other people." She's a God-fearing Christian who openly and proudly loves her gay fans, a Nashville icon imitated by drag queens, a honky-tonk performer sampled by rappers. Dolly Parton, simply, might be the last thing that all Americans have in common.

Think of the way she mythologizes coming up with her signature look—big boobs, red lips, tight skirts—which she has long claimed is modeled on a "tramp" she saw in town as a child. As she tells it, her mother disparaged the woman by calling her "trash," and Dolly cheekily replied with a smile: "Well, mama, I want to look like trash!" "We were really redneck, roughneck, hillbilly people. And I'm proud of it," she told *Southern Living* magazine in 2014. "That keeps you humble; that keeps you good." She has been honored by the Kennedy Center and performed for U.S. Presidents, but even then, she makes a joke out of her rags-to-riches trajectory: "There's nothing like white trash at the White House!" goes a quote long attributed to her.

Populism has been a buzzword in this election season, but compare Dolly's pleasant brand of it to the way Donald Trump has campaigned for president by playing on the very real economic worries of rural and small-town poor. As Trump leaves his skyscraper in Manhattan

to travel the country in his private jet, meeting voters in Iowa and New Hampshire and Ohio, I'm struck by how his outsider's view of the so-called "real America" has led him to come up with answers that are the polar opposite of what I hear on "Coat of Many Colors." He blames Muslims and immigrants instead of trying to come up with practical solutions. He stokes xenophobic fears and paranoia instead of trying to find something—anything—hopeful. Of course, it will take more than songs and platitudes to fix painful realities, but it's hard to comprehend how Dolly, who really was rural and impoverished, sees so much possibility in the ideas behind "Coat of Many Colors," where Trump, a city boy with a big leg up, only sees anger and hate.

The greatest testament to the Dolly school of politics was on display at a recent concert in Forest Hills, Queens, not so far from where Trump was born and raised. She played eight instruments throughout the night (all of them adorned with rhinestones), sang songs that hit notes of God and country in between playful pop hits like "9 to 5," and told many stories about her life growing up in Tennessee. In a medley of cover songs that would play well on both sides of the Mason-Dixon, she performed "The Night They Drove Old Dixie Down," a song by the Band told empathetically from the vantage point of a defeated Confederate soldier, and Bob Dylan's "Blowin' in the Wind," which became a Civil Rights anthem in the 1960s. And she sang "Coat of Many Colors," with a touch of sincerity so potent it was hard not to see it as an alternate national anthem, a powerful dash of foundational American folklore.

As the concert went on, I began to see Dolly as a hopeful bridge between conservative and liberal, Northern and

Southern, rural and urban. Throughout her career, she's been careful never to endorse a candidate for president, aware, I would guess, that her audience is a sensitive, tenuous mix. In fact, I had the opportunity to speak with her a few weeks after the concert about a new studio album, her 43rd, and she more or less said that she thought neither Hillary Clinton nor Trump seemed to care enough about the "good old American people." I couldn't disagree.

During the show, she defused the political tensions of the summer by joking that maybe what the White House needed more than anything was "more boobs!" before pointing to her own. Though part of me went into the night hoping she'd disavow Trump, revealing with her authentic country bonafides what a horrible phony he is, she didn't. But I eventually realized that her evasion of party politics could be a wonderful thing: Though we have come to see our political identities in concrete terms, with only one of two options available, Dolly is neither, at least to the public. It's comforting that she's just Dolly, and Dolly is for everyone.

So "Coat of Many Colors" is just about the prettiest little song you ever could hear and a balm in trying times. But what can we really learn from it? Perhaps the notion that "one is only poor only if they choose to be" is naive to the realities of hardship and poverty. But greeting even the worst things in the world with an ear for how we could be better—more modest, less judgmental, more loving—is a decent jumping-off point, especially when nothing else seems to be getting us any closer to the people we want to be. Dolly is the best of us, proof that there's still something good and worthwhile in these fractured 50 states. It might not be enough to stitch us all back together into some kind of Technicolor dream country, but right now, all we've got is a box of rags, and someone's got to start sewing. ✑

of change

N.W.A., "FUCK THA POLICE"
Sam Esmail

Creator of USA Network's "Mr. Robot"

I was 11 years old, an Egyptian-American growing up in South Carolina and then North Carolina, and there was a lot of racism. I remember hearing that song and I never took it literally, I just felt it was hugely empowering—and not just for minorities, but for anybody who felt misjudged or mistreated by authority. My favorite line is, "Yo, Dre, I got something to say." Then there's that beat, then there's "Fuck tha police." That was the other thing I loved about N.W.A.—and particularly that song—how raw and unpolished it felt. They just were so wild and young and unfiltered and brave. That they would reflect their experiences so honestly moves me in a way I don't think any other song has.

KRS-ONE, "SOUND OF THE POLICE"
Anders Holm

Costar and cocreator of Comedy Central's "Workaholics"

It's a song that you can turn way the fuck up and have a good time to, but it also calls absolute bullshit on the behavior of a lot of police officers—and then also goes into the systemic culture of police and African Americans. Also, "Girls Just Want to Have Fun" by Cyndi Lauper. Can't we just let the girls have fun?

DENISE HO'S *UNSTOPPABLE* ENERGY

FOR ALL THE RECENT RISE OF POLITICAL ACTIVISM IN MUSIC, NOT MANY GLOBAL POP STARS HAVE VOICED THEIR BELIEFS AT SUCH GREAT PERSONAL RISK AS **DENISE HO.**

BY MARC HOGAN

HO IS A MAJOR POP STAR IN HER NATIVE HONG KONG. KNOWN BY HER STAGE NAME, HOCC, THE 39-YEAR-OLD IS FAMOUS FROM THEATER, TV, AND FILM AS WELL AS FROM HER FROM HER MULTIPLE-AWARD-WINNING ALBUMS & ARENA-FILLING CONCERTS. SINCE 2010, SHE HAS ALSO RELEASED MUSIC IN MANDARIN, MAINLAND CHINA'S OFFICIAL LANGUAGE.

IN 1988, AT AGE 11, HO MOVED WITH HER FAMILY TO MONTREAL, WHERE SHE STAYED UNTIL AFTER COLLEGE, EXPERIENCING FIRSTHAND QUEBEC'S 1995

PHOTO BY ESTHER LEUNG

INDEPENDENCE REFERENDUM. HO WENT BACK TO HONG KONG IN 1996, WINNING A SINGING CONTEST AND KICKSTARTING HER MUSIC CAREER. THE NEXT YEAR, CHINA TOOK OVER THE TERRITORY FROM BRITAIN. THE GOVERNMENT IN BEIJING PROMISED TO GIVE PEOPLE IN HONG KONG FREEDOMS UNAVAILABLE IN THE MAINLAND, UNDER THE PRINCIPLE OF "ONE COUNTRY, TWO SYSTEMS." THAT IS, AT LEAST UNTIL 2047.

In the meantime, Ho has stood out as one of the island's most prominent champions of such civil liberties. Her work has long addressed traditionally sensitive social issues, from homosexuality on early hits like 2002's "Goodbye Rosemary" and in her 2005 stage musical *Butterfly Lovers*, to mental health on her 2008 album *Ten Days in the Madhouse*. In 2012, Ho became the first mainstream female singer in Hong Kong to come out as "tongzhi," a Chinese term for a gay person, and she has actively advocated LGBT rights. But she never officially ran afoul of China's long-ruling Communist Party.

Then, in 2014, Ho was one of the first celebrities arrested for demonstrating in the city's pro-democracy protests, called the Umbrella Movement or Occupy Central. From that point on, a de facto ban on Ho performing in mainland China has cost her a reported 80 percent of her old income. Ho did

nothing to return herself to the good graces of the authorities when, in May of this year, she posted a picture on Facebook of herself with the Dalai Lama. Ho called the Tibetan spiritual leader "my most respected teacher," though to Party leaders, he's a "wolf in monk's robes."

Soon after that, a state-run tabloid raised questions about French cosmetics company Lancôme sponsoring a Ho concert in Hong Kong. The event's billing: "Made of Unstoppable Energy." Lancôme quickly canceled, blaming its decision on "possible safety reasons," but it's surely no coincidence that China is the second biggest market for the brand's parent company, L'Oreal. On June 19, the same day and in the same location of the original performance, Ho instead performed for free, to a throng of peaceful audience members.

Braver still, Ho's civil disobedience comes at a time when Xi Jinping, the Communist Party chief since 2012, has been cracking down on political dissent. Late last year, five Hong Kong booksellers disappeared, apparently abducted by Chinese agents. In July, Hong Kong saw the first criminal convictions for student leaders of the 2014 pro-democracy demonstrations. In August, a human rights lawyer and three activists were found guilty of "subverting state power" in trials in the northeastern Chinese city of Tianjin.

Candidates in the September elections to Hong Kong's legislature had to sign a document declaring the territory an "inalienable part" of China—and formally disavowing the idea of independence. Nevertheless, six people who won seats to the 70-member council want Hong Kong to be more independent from the mainland. Their victories mark the first hint of separatism in a Chinese political institution since the Dalai Lama went into exile in 1959.

Espousing the "power of the individual," Ho spoke to TPR about her clash with Lancôme, the role of art in political protests, Lady Gaga, and a world war of the mind.

37

After Lancôme canceled your event together, what was the free concert you put on independently like?

DH   It was really touching, because so many people came. It was quite a narrow street and up on a hillside. There were almost 3,000 people who came to the show that day. Before we reorganized, I made contact with all the shops that were supposed to participate in Lancôme's original event. Most of them were so enthusiastic to join. It was a demonstration of how individuals, and individual shops, can do the same event, even without a very big corporation's help.

At the show, you said that people in Hong Kong and mainland China "have to fight for the basic human rights, which are freedom of speech and freedom of thought."

Freedom of speech in Hong Kong has been quite suppressed after the Umbrella Movement. It's really quite ridiculous. For me, and for many in Hong Kong, we are just speaking out for the basic human right to stand up for our beliefs without being punished. But this is getting really difficult right now in Hong Kong. Brands are silencing themselves because they have different things to lose if they stand up. I always say that I'm not a celebrity anymore; I'm more like an activist. Many other people from the entertainment industry do not have the choice.

What power do singers have to effect change?

Hong Kong hasn't ever been in a situation like this before. Hong Kong is a materialistic society, and capitalistic [laughs] society. Even in 1989, when we had one million people on the streets for the Beijing students [pro-democracy demonstrators killed in the Tiananmen Square Massacre], that was for people elsewhere. So

I always say that Hong Kongers are quite green in this area: We are starting to participate in social movements and to fight for our own rights.

But that's a question that arose during the Umbrella Movement: "What is the use of songs and art in such a difficult time?" There were some youngsters against people singing during the movement, because they think it's showing weakness. For me, that's a misunderstanding of art and music. But that is an understandable [misconception]: In Hong Kong, music never served the purpose of talking about social issues; it was always for entertainment—love songs and all that. But for me personally, music is a very important way to solidify different beliefs and to encourage people. I think that is one of the ways we can get messages through. Now so much information is flying everywhere and just comes and goes. But music and the arts are there to stay. If you put your beliefs into the process of making your music, I think that is what can be preserved, especially in such a crazy time.

It's not only a crazy time for Hong Kong; it's a crazy time for the whole world. When we think about various moments in history, most of the time we can refer to the songs that came out in those eras. Like, say, Bob Dylan or John Lennon—the way they put their messages into the songs, that is very, very important. I think that's the original purpose of making music: to record the history that is happening at the same time as when the singer has made that song, or to preserve all sorts of beliefs into the words and the melody. As a singer who is going through such a particular time in Hong Kong, it's one of my responsibilities to put these feelings and these experiences into my own work.

HO PERFORMS A FREE SHOW ON JUNE 19 IN HONG KONG—THE SAME DATE AND LOCATION OF LANCÔME'S CANCELLED SPONSORSHIP. PHOTO BY ESTHER LEUNG

"TECHNOLOGY IS MAKING PEOPLE DIVIDED—NOT ONLY IN HONG KONG, BUT EVERYWHERE."

Have you experienced pressure from the government?
They never actually do it openly, in the public [laughs]. But they have all kinds of propaganda. My incident with Lancôme happened because [Chinese government mouthpiece *Global Times*] started asking people, "What do you think about this singer who has spoken out against the Chinese government? What do you think about Lancôme cooperating with her?"

Also, corporations have pressure from behind the scenes. We cannot see it, but I have heard many stories about record companies taking calls from the Chinese government, asking them to ask their artists to shut up [laughs]. These things are really happening.

Just recently, there was a Taiwanese actor [Leon Dai] and a Japanese actress [Kiko Mizuhara] participating in a Chinese movie [the romantic comedy *No Other Love*]. Because the Taiwanese actor supported a pro-democracy movement in Taiwan and also in Hong Kong, he was forced to openly apologize. The Japanese actress liked a photo of [Chinese dissident artist] Ai Weiwei, so she also had to shoot a video apology to the Chinese citizens. That sort of thing is happening in places besides Hong Kong: It's happening in Taiwan; it's happening to Japanese artists trying to get into the Chinese market.

Lancôme is a French company. Even a company from France succumbs to this kind of pressure. It's not one particular incident; it's affecting show business worldwide. Even Lady Gaga [laughs]: I don't know if you saw the news, but she met the Dalai Lama, and because of this, Chinese newspapers were saying, "Oh, she's going to be banned in China."

What are the challenges of standing up for LGBT rights in Hong Kong?
It's difficult. The Legislative Council is the only government department Hong Kong people can elect directly, but there is another section elected by the Hong Kong government. So when we are trying to push for different amendments, they are most frequently blocked by the people who are pro-government. LGBT rights can never go through, because they have this army of candidates in the Legislative Council that try to ban everything the government is against. So it's a very difficult situation in Hong Kong, not only for LGBT rights, but also for minorities and for older people—they're trying get the rights for pensions, and it's not going through. But all the things that are pro-government,

even if it's spending all amounts of money, all go through. That's why the Umbrella Movement happened in 2014, because we are asking to elect our own chief executive. As long as we cannot elect the chief executive, it's always going to be like this.

Was it a shock in 2014 when the police started responding forcibly to the protests? That hadn't happened before, right?
Yeah, it's awakened a lot of Hong Kong people. Because before it was like, "These are not issues that affect Hong Kong people directly"—even though they were. But the tear gas, and what happened in 2014, has enraged a lot of Hong Kong people. Since then, people are trying very hard to fight, but it's difficult. So for me, one of the few celebrities who can speak out—it's what I have to do.

What's next? I understand that you're crowdfunding a concert this fall.
I have my Hong Kong concert in October. I was calling for sponsors because the normal way—well, "normal," the classic way of doing it in Hong Kong—is you try to find a few big corporations to sponsor your concert, say for one million dollars, and you can ensure a budget. But because no corporations would dare to approach me, I tried to transform this tradition of doing concerts. I divided this big sponsor into many, many small portions, so smaller companies can join in—and individuals even. So it is like crowdfunding, but the term I use is a "collective, exclusive sponsorship." [Laughs] I got a really good response, because every unit is an amount of 15,000 Hong Kong dollars and I had over 200-something people who applied. I actually got more sponsorship than I would have if I only called for corporations. This is my way to encourage Hong Kong citizens that we do not need to depend on corporations to survive. We can survive on our own, by standing together.

For the concert itself, I am trying to address issues that are not only about Hong Kong. The whole situation that is happening everywhere in the world, I'm quite concerned: all the terrorist attacks, the elections in the States, and the Brexit. Technology is making people quite divided—not only in Hong Kong, but everywhere. For our team, we think the whole world is entering in a different sort of world war. I don't know if you would agree with me, but all that is happening in the world, it's quite heavy for us. The main theme of our concert is anti-war—but it's another sort of war: It's not the war with guns and heavy weapons; it's a war of the mind, and that is even more terrifying for me. ✑

PINK, "DEAR MR. PRESIDENT"
Denise Ho

I sang "Dear Mr. President" at the end of a concert last year. When Pink wrote that song [in 2006], it was addressing George [W.] Bush, but I think it's applicable anywhere in the world. When I sang that song, I was addressing the chairman of China—I didn't say it at the time, but I had this in mind. Because I believe every person still has a side of humanity. Obviously, for some, it's overshadowed by power, but I believe that every person was born pure, but because of what people go through, they head in different directions. I think it's important to remind people that whether you are the president of a country or just a normal citizen, you can do what you can [to effect change]. ✑

SONGS OF CHANGE
Interviews by Marc Hogan
and Camille Dodero

THE SOUND

OF
YOUNG
AMERICA

They were a self-identified terrorist group playing a kinetic scramble of garage, jazz, and punk. They advocated **REVOLUTION**, endorsed **HICKEYS**, and **DISAGREED WITH SLEEP.**

Were D.C. underground favorites the **NATION OF ULYSSES** a post-hardcore band or a fringe political party? Twenty-five years later, they're still **SOMETHING ENTIRELY ELSE.**

BY MARC MASTERS
PHOTOS BY MICHAEL GALINSKY

IN THE 1990S, A NUMBER OF AMERICAN PUNK AND INDIE ROCK BANDS MADE MUSIC YOU COULD CALL "POLITICAL."

But none of them were like the Nation of Ulysses. Formed in Washington, D.C., near the end of the 1980s, this five-piece post-hardcore act burst forth in the underground with a fully-formed worldview, complex ideology, and sharply defined set of sonic and visual aesthetics.

The Nation of Ulysses lived together in a house called The Embassy, dressed in matching outfits, and blared a chaotic scramble of punk, garage, noise, and jazz. But unlike most bands, they identified as a "violent separatist political party and terrorist group," touting official slogans ("The Nation of Ulysses Must Prevail") and chants ("Ulysses, Ulysses, little flower, beloved by all the youth"). The liner notes to their five releases —three albums and two 7" singles—delivered bullet-pointed manifestos and advocated revolutionary acts. *Ulysses Speaks*, their self-published zine and official "party organ," dove even deeper into an apparently bottomless well of rhetorical jargon.

"The group began as an idea," Ian Svenonius—singer, trumpet player, and designated NOU "mouthpiece"—says today. "It started as something political and poetic—an ideology and a platform, basically—rather than as a rock'n'roll band. We were trying to create a new vocabulary, a new culture." Even more ambitiously, he admits, "We were trying to create a nation."

For Svenonius and his four musical comrades, this was a form of protest. But rather than dole out political messages in overly earnest tones, they preferred to baffle, to amuse, and to disorient. They proselytized like a life-altering cult and obfuscated like an absurdist art collective; they pledged allegiance to both revolution and candy. It was art as politics, but even more so, politics as art—with a ton more going on between the two.

"In the American independent underground scene," Svenonius insists, "The Nation of Ulysses really had no precedent." They also had no real descendents—and that might be the most confusing part.

"The construction of
the Ulyssean sound
and liberation begins on
the ruins of music and
especially rock'n'roll....
On the rubble of that dead
city we shall erect a futurist
construction of noise."

—The liner notes to the NOU's second album,
Plays Pretty For Baby

Issue No. 009

THE PARTY ORGAN FOR THE NATION OF ULYSSES

THE 1990s were rife with retread punk bands offering little intellectual weight or distinctive style. "What was called hardcore was very formulaic," says Ian MacKaye, who toured with the NOU frequently as the frontman of Fugazi. "Both of [our bands] tried to confront that formula."

At the time, the rock band as self-contained, all-encompassing entity was not unprecedented. Take Devo's uniformed, army-like "devolution." Or the hermetic, iconographic world created by the anonymous Residents. Or the MC5's left-wing sloganeering and involvement in the anti-racist White Panther Party. Svenonius offers Slovenian industrial outfit Laibach—formed in 1980 and branded dissidents at home—as an antecedent to "the group as political party, a detached and almost impersonal mouthpiece for ideology."

Uniquely positioned to devise a new punk worldview, Svenonius grew up in Hyattsville, Md., to parents who both had doctorates in philosophy. He went to art school in D.C., but the comic books he drew there were "mostly narratives about revolution," he told the *Washington Post* in 1990.

In cocreating the NOU's confrontational stance, the frontman and his bandmates found inspiration in the 1920s Surrealist movement and its 1960s offshoot, the Situationist International. Both subverted convention through confusion and contradiction, using avant-garde art to critique traditions and institutions. These influences dovetailed with the NOU's fixation on radical political organizations, like the New People's Army, the guerrilla arm of the Philippines' communist party whose revolutionary fighters the band called "excellent role models" in its 1991 song "P. Power." The

sensuousness to square society. To quote Raoul Vaneigem, "People who talk about revolution and class struggle without referring explicitly to everyday life, without understanding what is subversive about love and what is positive in the refusal of constraints, such people have a corpse in their mouth."
CURRENCY: During the decline of Babylon Capitalism, the Nation's currency exchange rates with the money notes of the old world have rendered such transactions as buying and selling as passé or obsolete. Thusly, the N.O. Ulysses urges the dismemberment of the old market economy through indiscriminate pilfering which should give way in turn to rampant looting. "What are you waiting for? TAKE THE KINGDOM OF HEAVEN BY STORM."
NATION: Nation indicates common-visioned army of the new Ulysses underworld and does not indicate either "rock 'N' roll group" (passé) or "state" (Off The Pigs!). The Nation of Ulysses begets its lineage not from musical bands, but from terrorist gorups and political parties. The term "Nation" implies self-construciton of the highest order beyond the old r 'n' r tradition of renaming one's self and into a new wilderland of complete rejection of the dictates of parent-culture laws/hegemony. We declare the Zero Generation (the destruction of the past) and cast off the restraints of precedence and history which would attempt to define our limitless and explosive revolution in their own failed terms. We declare our age as 18 as we refuse the reins and chains of work ethic responsibility, and align ourselves with the N.O.U. boys and girls klub BACKPACK STAR KIDS PLAY BALL!

ULYSSES SPEAKS, ISSUE 9 | COURTESY OF DISCHORD RECORDS

45

Nation of Islam also had an impact on the NOU, who named their followers the FOU (Fruit of Ulysses), a nod to the Fruit of Islam, the Nation of Islam's paramilitary wing.

NOU actually self-identified as "a terrorist group," something that perhaps raised fewer eyebrows—and less concern for national security—in 1990 than it would in a post-9/11 U.S. (When asked whether that self-identification ever gave him pause, MacKaye says it was "obviously a joke.") But even as a metaphor, the idea of terror was powerful for Svenonius. "We were more influenced by a kind of absurdist terror—like the idea of art terror." Some of the NOU literature was modeled on a CIA manual Svenonius found called "Terror Group Profiles," using it as guidebook to, as he puts it, "make the best composite terror group."

From these sources, the NOU crafted a rich worldview where sincerity levels were uncertain. For one thing, the group never committed any literal acts of terror. For another, much of this merchandise-slash-propaganda was unmistakably laughable, like the facetious liner notes tracing members' supposed outlaw histories: Guitarist Steve Kroner "was arrested for having a bomb in his luggage" in Amsterdam and "later deported to Japan"; bassist Steve Gamboa was dubbed "the little lamb of Ulysses" due to his "purity of intention"; guitarist Tim Green supposedly quit the seminary due to the siren call of the NOU; and drummer James Canty was touted in NOU literature as "physically remarkable for a wooden leg [and] a single kidney."

"It's hard to talk about [their philosophy] because it wasn't really tongue-in-cheek," says MacKaye, whose Dischord label released two of the band's albums. "But in a way, it was."

Some of their general philosophies were clear, though. They sought to reclaim a youth-based counterculture overtaken by "square" institutions, including what they saw as the dying form of rock'n'roll. They advocated secession from America to create a nation which would "recognize youth as a class," insisting that "for political reasons, [members'] ages will not change from 18." ("That was because 18-year-olds have no power, no agency," explains Svenonius, who himself was only 19 when the NOU formed. "So it was saying, 'This group will give you agency. Join our ranks as a youth class.' It was saying you can elect to be outside of adult responsibility.")

In positing their new youth-culture state, the Nation of Ulysses crafted humorously odd dictums delineating actions their followers should take. Many of these repurposed and reframed tenets of childhood and teen culture, giving them new, surprising, possibly ridiculous rationales. For example, they recommended binging on sweets ("In the strategic use of sugar, Ulysses encourages the state of manic exaltation"), worshipping Halloween ("A potent instrument for revolt, with its tradition of... house-to-house looting if demands for candy are not immediately satiated"), and branding fellow young people with hickeys ("Our badge of courage shall be the bruise of passion inflicted by our loved ones").

They even insisted that Nation members forgo sleep altogether. "While society sleeps, bound to this archaic ritual, we shall take over," a two-page essay included in the first NOU album, 1991's *13-Point Program To Destroy America*, explained. "Sleep wipes away a lot of inhibitions which could stymie one's fever toward the destruction of the false nation and toward construction of the new."

It's unclear whether NOU acolytes ever took these as serious, literal guidelines—or whether the band itself actually followed them. "I once had an argument with them, because they said they don't believe in sleep," MacKaye says. "I said, 'You just don't believe in going to bed early. You guys sleep all fucking day.'"

Svenonius insists that the NOU meant it all. "We were definitely being didactic," he says. "That was the idea."

WE

CONF

THE

DECLARE

ISION

"They
confused
people"
—Ian MacKaye

NEW   RULE

> **"We begin with fashion because we believe that each ensemble which one wears has its place in an internal system of differences... and fits a corresponding set of socially prescribed roles and options."**
>
> *—Ulysses Speaks*

To the Nation of Ulysses, presentation was as important as sound, speech, and message. Every visual element—colors, fonts, clothing, hair—was a carefully chosen part of the package. "If you look at the success of Bolshevism, where would they be without the color red?" says Svenonius. "It's not just what you say; it's the way that you say it."

Their sartorial flair—usually retro-styled suits and ties—was another way to confront the band's staid milieu. In '90s punk, looking sharp was so rare that it was practically a sin. "We didn't understand the hierarchy: Why sound over fashion?" Svenonius asks. "When punk started, you could say that it was actually a fashion trend—the music was in a sense the secondary consideration. The Sex Pistols started as models for a clothing shop. For us, fashion was central and important in creating a new culture."

"Hardcore had gotten so unstylish," says Calvin Johnson, whose K label released the first NOU 7" jointly with Dischord. "People used to dress up to go to shows, but then somehow it became punk to be bland. Just the fact that [the NOU] were saying that it's desirable to have a sense of style—that was a political statement." Johnson's band Beat Happening toured multiple times with the NOU, connecting on another aspect of stage presentation. "We both had the idea that dancing was the point of music."

Dancing earned an official plank in the NOU platform. "The significance of angularity in elbows and knees cannot be downplayed when Ulysses engages in our tight and kinetic boy/girl interplay," *Ulysses Speaks* declared. Or, as Svenonius sung in the anthem "The Sound of Young America": "This is the sound that's around/That keeps me dancing in my room/It's illicit, cool, and out of tune."

The Nation of Ulysses insisted that they made "sound, not music." Though their structured songs drew heavily from earlier garage music, they always allowed room for chaos. The goal was to create an atmosphere of revolution by enveloping listeners with what 13-Point Program to Destroy America's opening song title called "Spectra Sonic Sound"— aka "the sound that surrounds," as one lyric put it. Inside that sound, Svenonius' lyrics flipped rock clichés, another step in using youth culture to build principles of a political nation. "A Kid Who Tells on Another Kid Is a Dead Kid" grafted playground code onto rules of warfare. "Hickey Underworld" implored followers to "put your lips to my neck for a key to the action index." "You're My Miss Washington D.C." espoused the idea of a never-ending weekend as a way to "exonerate us from... the wage system and the work week." It was all about reclaiming a culture and making it new again: In "Hot Chocolate City," Svenonius sang, "We built it/Let's take it over/We started it/Let's start another."

On record, these songs were kinetic and hyperac-

51

tive; in concert, they verged on what the group called "a blanket of noise" made with discordant guitars, caffeinated beats, and Svenonius' revival-tent screams. The sight and sound of five young men in smashing suits, throbbing around to garage-rock-gone-haywire, seemed meant to baffle anyone accustomed to the then-prevalent rules of punk.

"There's no question they confused people," recalls MacKaye. "Their shows were so chaotic and confrontational. They were basically saying, 'We are us and not you.' That was part of their aesthetic: They were separate. But the energy was undeniable."

"We stand poised on the edge of history, awaiting the end of music with optimism."

—The liner notes to *Plays Pretty For Baby*

PHILOSOPHICALLY the Nation of Ulysses stood outside their own time. But in practice, they fit in, befriending and touring with scores of sympathetic punk bands. Both Svenonius and MacKaye point to the riot grrrl movement as kindred spirits—particularly in the way they also used presentation to make points: Riot grrrl pioneers Bikini Kill toured with the NOU; some members lived in The Embassy for a time; and all contributed vocals to *Plays Pretty for Baby*. But the NOU's lasting influence is harder to discern. A decade later, European bands like Refused, The (International) Noise Conspiracy, and The Hives borrowed the NOU's fashion sense and stage swagger, though they mostly eschewed politics for pure entertainment.

In many ways, the best carrier of the Nation of Ulysses flame is Svenonius himself. After NOU disbanded in late 1992, he formed The Make-Up, which included NOU compatriots Canty and Gamboa and forged new paths with the same spiritual mission. "Instead of politics, we'd use religion," he recalls. "Instead of the political party, we'll go into the church—so we created a non-religious sermon band." Svenonius has continued to merge art, philosophy, and politics through subsequent groups (Chain & The Gang, Weird War), as well as his uniquely thought-provoking essays and books.

Today, in a time when political discourse is dominated by simplicities and nuance has become nearly anachronistic, why it's surprising that few rock groups like the Nation of Ulysses have risen up as a corrective. Svenonius wonders if such a thing is even possible today. "Making a group is different now," he says. "It's seen as another thing to put on a résumé. Nation of Ulysses was never that kind of thing. It was total devotion and immersion in something that was pretty inscrutable to people outside of it. People's imagination about what's possible is different now. Life is less theoretical because there's less time for theory—everything's just maintaining. There's no respite. You can't read a book if you're just constantly reading email."

Svenonius' point hints at a larger issue: the way the internet has usurped music as a locus for discourse and protest. Perhaps the reason there are few groups today as stubbornly immersive as the Nation of Ulysses is that it's quicker and more effective to spread political viewpoints online. In that sense, spending time and energy building a complex, comprehensive worldview through music might seem antiquated. But as long as you're starting a band, why not make it be about something?

"What they really celebrated was new ideas," says MacKaye. "I hope that the same way people draw inspiration from any great movement, they would see the Nation of Ulysses in that lineage—as people who dared to act on a new idea." ✍

53

A PERSONAL JOURNEY THROUGH UK POLITICS AND POP

THE RIP IT UP AND START AGAIN AUTHOR LOOKS AT HOW MUSIC DID (AND DID NOT) SHAPE HIS HOME COUNTRY

BY SIMON REYNOLDS

SEX PISTOLS "ANARCHY IN THE U.K.";
"GOD SAVE THE QUEEN" (1977)

I first heard the Sex Pistols in mid-1978, a full year after "God Save the Queen" convulsed the United Kingdom in the summer of '77. Living in a small English town far from the action, my 14-year-old head was elsewhere all through '77, sideways glimpsing punk's existence only in photo spreads of outrageous haircuts in Sunday newspaper magazines. When I finally heard *Never Mind the Bollocks*, the Pistols' story affected me as a rock-myth fait accompli, rather than unfolding as a real-time historical sequence with an uncertain outcome.

It was my brother Tim—a few years younger, far better endowed in street cred because he went to a state school—who brought home a cassette of songs by the Pistols and Ian Dury & the Blockheads and later bought *Bollocks*. Because I wasn't going to gigs yet, or reading the music press—and was only rarely seeing groups like these on TV—punk's power manifested itself to me almost entirely as sheer sonic force: I'd never heard anything so domineering, never even imagined that "pop" could be this unbridled—such an attack.

The record covers were thrilling too, thanks to punk's aggressively innovative graphic language (*Bollocks*' ransom-note newsprint lettering, for instance). But most of all, it was the voices in punk, a kind never heard before in pop: tones of jubilant bitterness; a sense of malevolent power conjured up from within the singer's body through sheer will and blasted at the listener. The voice, above all, of Johnny Rotten. That, and the things he sang about. Like anarchy, an intoxicating and unfamiliar concept.

It's moot whether "Anarchy in the U.K." should be taken as a Political Statement; it's more like prophecy or poetry. If the song corresponds to any ideology, the closest thing is the 19th century stripe of anarchism associated with German philosopher Max Stirner, who imagined the state being dissolved in favor of a "union of egoists." Anarchy, in this worldview, means absolute sovereignty for each individual, who's no longer subject to higher authority or constraints on the free exercise of desire. Anarchism, in other words, that has nothing to do with the placid, orderly decision-making of communes or workers' councils; rather, it's an apocalyptic unleashing, a chaos of wills, with each individual ruling his or her life like a tyrant. That's how I hear the chorus "I wanna be/Anarchy," which Rotten drags out like a triumphant jeer.

As a vision for how society should organize itself, "Anarchy in the U.K." is literally puerile, the sort of thoughts entertained by adolescents with no inkling of how challenging life is. But I was 15 when I heard the song. The Pistols spoke most intoxicatingly to boys between 13 and 17: a period in life when you have an innate flair for recklessness, an awesome ability to disregard consequences. Boredom—and something darker too, an appetite for destruction—drove the brothers Reynolds and our peers towards vandalism, risk-taking ("dares"), and pranks. It's the nastiness of punk—the "I wanna destroy" side, the Vicious-ness—that gets written out of the validating histories, which invariably accentuate punk's idealism, the empowering and constructive do-it-yourself ethos. But in our suburban bedroom, we thrilled to the tales of the Pistols puking at airports, Sid slashing his chest onstage, and the seductively cynical notion that it had always been a swindle, a Malcolm McLaren cash-from-chaos master plan.

Age 20 when he recorded "Anarchy," Rotten was already a bit old for this kind of thing—and in truth, he wasn't a "Smash It Up" punk at heart, but a book-reading, record-collecting hipster who shrank from real-life violence. McLaren, at 30, should have been well past this way of thinking. But the Pistols' manager idealized, venerated, and also envied, teenagers as the only really revolutionary class. Existing in a liminal limbo between childhood and duty-bound adulthood, emboldened by the dawning sense of their own physical and mental independence,

the Kids were the only ones who could ever change things, because they had no stakes in the status quo.

Where "Anarchy" is timeless Gnostic-Romantic poetry, "God Save the Queen" diminishes itself slightly by being topical, as well as having the shape of a Classic Rock Anthem. The historical peg was the Royal Jubilee celebration of Queen Elizabeth's 25 years on the throne, "a mad parade" of imperial nostalgia that covered every town in Britain with bunting and Union Jacks. The Pistols' single was such an affront—the lyric described the monarchy as a "fascist regime"—that the song led not just to a BBC ban, but to enraged patriots violently assaulting members of the band. Despite the embargo, the single reached No. 2 on the UK chart; some believe that devious conniving by the authorities kept "Queen" off the top spot to save further embarrassment to The Establishment.

The scandal of "God Save the Queen" set up impossible expectations for what politics in pop could achieve. It restored a belief in rock's power to incite and to threaten that had waned steadily since the heyday of The Stones and The Who. But it was "Anarchy in the U.K.," and other *Bollocks* songs like "Bodies"—a foaming fulmination, explosive with expletives, against the horror of human biological existence—that set the true challenge for rock going forward: How to equal the expressive force of a voice, and a sound, that felt so corrosive it would surely shake the world? The Sex Pistols songs were rock's equivalent to the theses nailed by Luther on the Wittenberg church door: They made a decisive break with the Old Wave, while also—like the Reformation before it—opening the way for further schisms, the proliferation of sects pursuing different ideas of what punk now meant and how that dramatically revivified power should be deployed most righteously.

TOM ROBINSON BAND "POWER IN THE DARKNESS"; "TRB 2" (1978-9)

The only fan of Tom Robinson Band I ever knew was a boy in my lower-sixth class (equivalent to the 11th grade) called Sandbrook, who had daubed TRB's clenched-fist stencil-style logo onto his satchel. His satchel also bore the insignias for Rock Against Racism and the Anti-Nazi

League, other indicators of simpatico values that stood out at a school where: 1) The Conservatives always won the mock elections; and 2) A friend's parents declared that the world should quit meddling in South Africa's affairs, because the system there worked well for everybody—and they weren't hounded out of polite society.

Speaking of sides, one of TRB's anthems was titled "Better Decide Which Side You're On." Tom Robinson conceived of his band's constituency as a rainbow coalition of the disadvantaged and marginalized: the unemployed, racial minorities, gays, squatters, feminists, drug users. In reality, TRB's following was largely composed of progressive-minded white middle-class youth, very much in the mold of Robinson himself—a clean-cut, well-spoken, smiley chap who came over as earnest, unthreatening, and "straight" (although actually openly and vocally gay). Those who'd been energized by punk, but wanted something constructive and more clearly aligned in its left allegiances, rallied to TRB's banner.

Robinson's approach to music was means-to-an-end: He wanted to bring his message to as wide an audience as possible. Accordingly, TRB's rousing sound was rooted in the Old Wave more than the New Wave, finding a stomping, if stiff-hipped, groove midway between Free and Mott the Hoople. Well-played and cleanly produced, the road song "2-4-6-8 Motorway" was commercial enough to crack the Top 5. But the group's single and album covers were plastered with contacts for every imaginable pressure group and activist organisation.

TRB were huge in 1978: Critics hailed them as a positive realization of punk's promise, there was an hour-long TV documentary devoted to the band, and the tours took in ever-larger concert halls. But almost instantly the music press turned on them for "preaching to the converted" and for being too straight in their angle of address (lyrically and musically). Reaching the unconverted became a crucial concern going forward. But equally important for those looking both to live up to, and to extend, punk was the idea of challenging and unsettling the converted. Musicians and critics began to explore the idea that politics was not about the transmission and reception of messages but the initiation of a thought process. In the next stage, "question everything" and "personal politics" became key buzz concepts.

WHY WAS I SO DOWN ON PREACHING TO THE CONVERTED?

CRASS *STATIONS OF THE CRASS; "BLOODY REVOLUTIONS"; "OUR WEDDING" (1979-81)*

Crass, a collective of former hippies and new punks who lived in a communal farm cottage called Dial House, took the "anarchy" in "Anarchy in the U.K." literally. Punk, for them, was about self-rule. Crass opposed all forms of hierarchy: State, Army, Church. They brandished slogans like "Fight War Not Wars. Destroy Power Not People" and "You can't vote anarchist, you can only be one." Politics was "politricks" and a power game (another black-flag slogan was "Whoever you vote for, the government wins"). For Crass, the left was just as bad as the right: *Stations'* "White Punks on Hope" equated socialist violence and fascist violence as "just the same old game."

the anarcho-punk movement it spawned; Crass were also accused of puritanism and sloganeering.

Yet Crass had a mischievous side, a McLaren-like delight in the publicity stunt as a form of subversive media theatre. Most famous of their pranks was the Thatchergate hoax: a 1982 record purporting to be a telephone conversation between the British Prime Minister and Ronald Reagan, during which the allies revealed dirty secrets about the Falklands War and the President's plan for a showdown with the Soviets, using Europe as the arena of conflict. The intelligence services got in a right flap about it, with the U.S. State Department initially identifying the record as a KGB ruse. (As it turned out, Crass had spliced together bits from the leaders' public speeches to sound like a dialogue.) But the one that really tickled me was in 1981, when—in the guise of Creative Recording and Sound Services, which acronyms as C.R.A.S.S.—they persuaded Loving, a mushy romantic magazine aimed at young women, to run a special offer for the free flexi-single "Our Wedding." Sung by the band's second female singer, Joy De Vivre—to the accompaniment of strings, church organ, and wedding bells—this supposed celebration of marriage was really a sardonic poker-faced exposé of matrimony as mutual bondage: "Listen to those wedding bells/Say goodbye to other girls"; "Never look at anyone/Must be all you see." Hundreds wrote in for the flexi before a newspaper revealed the prank. Talking to *NME* in June 1981, the band's Penny Rimbaud railed at *Loving*-type magazines as "obscene and despicable rags" peddling "teenage pornography" that "trivialized love and relationships." (Perfectly in character, Crass later put the single on their 1981 album *Penis Envy*.)

My brothers were Crass fans and one single they played a great deal, 1980's "Bloody Revolutions," picked up this theme, criticizing macho hard-left militancy in the same way that John Lennon, in the Beatles' "Revolution," jeered at dogma-indoctrinated radicals with their Chairman Mao placards. At university in the early '80s, I encountered this divide within the anarchist community itself: gentle hippie-ish types largely concerned with getting their minds right (feminist consciousness-raising groups for both women and men) versus the hothead street guerrilla types happy to leave the chicks and the wimps to their navel-gazing and get down to serious business—like hurling bricks at the police.

Although their music got more sophisticated and experimental, early Crass treated sound as a mere delivery system for the messages. That was one reason the British music press initially scorned the group and

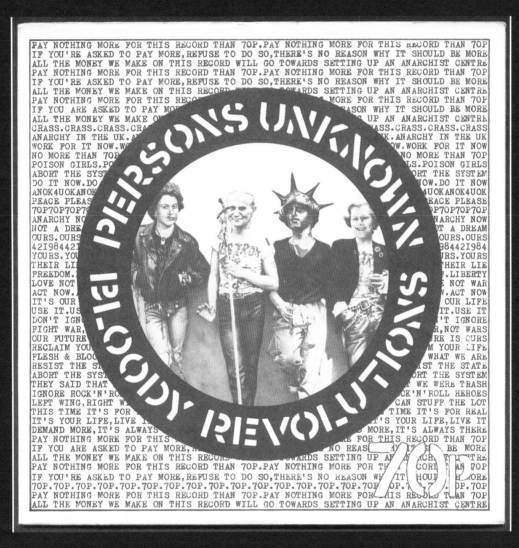

Virtually all Crass singles and LPs topped the UK's independent releases chart: Their following was huge, especially out in the provinces where punk achieved its greatest, and most lingering, impact a few years after London and Manchester had moved on musically and sartorially. You saw the Crass stencil all over the UK: on walls, on paving stones, and on the leather jackets of the punx mooching in clutches around bus shelters and the fountains outside town halls. For most of the fans— including my brothers—the appeal of Crass was as much to do with band's visuals as its rudimentary sonics. The records came in elaborate packaging that folded out to form posters featuring Gee Vaucher's beautifully drawn photo-realist counter-propaganda—dreamlike tableaus in which Thatcher and Queen Elizabeth were leather-clad punkettes, the Statue of Liberty had a Mohawk, and Pope John Paul II wore a "Destroy" T-shirt.

DEXYS MIDNIGHT RUNNERS *SEARCHING FOR THE YOUNG SOUL REBELS (1980)*

Post-punk hatched an ascetic streak latent in punk: a suspicion of pleasure for its own sake. Entertainment for its own sake was escapist, a narcotic—music needed to carry a higher purpose of consciousness-raising or critique. Sometimes accused of being didactic and dour, groups like Gang of Four, the Au Pairs, The Pop Group, and Scritti Politti were my kind of post-punk puritan, perfect for a young mind that was beginning to approach the world critically. But there was another kind of puritan around on the early-'80s British music scene: mod-influenced youth-leader types like The Jam's Paul Weller and Dexys Midnight Runners' Kevin Rowland.

Dexys retained and intensified punk's will-to-power— they are named after a brand of amphetamine, after all. Rowland's first response to punk had been The Killjoys, the name itself indicating a puritanical zeal seemingly at odds with his Irish Catholic background. Depressed in the aftermath of punk, Rowland rallied his spirits with the horn-pumping, muscular soul of '60s performers like Geno Washington. This became the template for Dexys' sound: brassy, uplifting, pugnacious. *Searching for the Young Soul Rebels*, the debut LP, starts with the sounds of a radio: Bursts of Sex Pistols and the Specials (another politics-in-pop byproduct of punk) are heard

amid the hiss and crackle, before Rowland's exasperated voice cries, "For God's sake, burn it down." Dexys set themselves up here as next in a series of insurgent renewals for British music. The LP title is an open call for recruits, an attempt to conjure a new youth movement out of nowhere.

The nature of "young soul rebellion" remained unclear, though. Political specifics figured here and there. "Dance Stance," the debut single, took issue with derogatory stereotypes about the Irish, defiantly reeling off the nation's list of illustrious literati. The LP cover featured a Catholic boy from Ulster being driven from his Belfast home during the sectarian clearances of 1971; one song concerned Rowland's unsuccessful attempt to set up a union at his workplace. But the overriding emphasis was on the internal politics of the British music scene, on Dexys' candidacy as a messianic force, and on Rowland's belief in, well, belief.

"There, There My Dear," the follow-up hit to the No. 1 "Geno," was a paranoid rejoinder to a journalist or musician who refused to "welcome the new soul vision." Almost thrown away in the accusatory bluster was one of political pop's most provocative thought-bombs: "The only way to change things is to shoot men who arrange things." The implication is that music can only ever be incidental to the struggle. But given that Rowland and his Dexys would carry on being pop stars, recording two more '80s albums before dispersing for a couple of decades, you might well draw a further inference: They are not really that interested in changing things. That raises the perturbing possibility: Is pop an arena in which those with the temperament of revolutionaries can experience all the self-aggrandizing excitement of leadership, without any of the unglamorous costs or consequences of actual struggle?

KATE BUSH *"BREATHING"*; UB40 *"THE EARTH DIES SCREAMING"*; FRANKIE GOES TO HOLLYWOOD *"TWO TRIBES" (1980-1984)*

It is almost impossible to convey to young people today what it was like to grow up during the '60s, '70s, and (first half of) the '80s, with the awareness that nuclear annihilation was a real prospect constantly hanging over you. One of my high school projects was a paper on the effects of a 10-megaton bomb dropping on London. Our hometown was about 35 miles from the capital's center —the bullseye in the target for Soviet bombs—and so it would escape the fireball and direct blast, but receive some very fierce winds followed by radioactive fallout. Around this time, I joined the Campaign for Nuclear Disarmament, which was then resurging after the government's consent to base U.S.-controlled cruise missiles on British soil, a decision that would turn the UK into a launchpad—and thus a prime target for Soviet retaliation, or a preemptive strike.

Pop picked up on these currents of anxiety with a string of songs about nuclear war. Kate Bush's disturbing, if overwrought, 1980 single "Breathing" described "chips of plutonium" penetrating the bloodstream shared by a pregnant mother and her unborn child. Despite the melodramatic title, UB40's hit "The Earth Dies Screaming" was even more chillingly subdued: Its dread bass and funereal pace turned the atmosphere ashen in the *Top of the Pops* studio.

A few years later came what was intended as the ultimate protest record: Frankie Goes to Hollywood's single "Two Tribes," a follow-up to "Relax," released by the arty-provocateur label ZTT. Lyrically inane and emotionally ambiguous (at times, it seemed almost to exult in Armageddon, the excitement of living in a world "where sex and horror are the new gods"), "Two Tribes" nonetheless brought the issue to the biggest possible audience, colonizing the No. 1 spot on the UK singles chart for nine weeks during the summer of 1984. The sleeves of its numerous 12-inch mixes resembled my school project, caked in data and diagrams about what a superpower showdown would entail for short-term lethality and long-term species extinction. (A brightly colored graph totted up the death toll in categories ranging from nuclear winter and famine to disease and psychological trauma.) Yet as ZTT's conceptualist Paul Morley noted wryly, "Two Tribes" was replaced, after two months atop the charts, by George Michael's "Careless Whisper." Nothing changed—not even in pop, let alone in the outside world.

THE STYLE COUNCIL "SHOUT TO THE TOP"; THE REDSKINS "KEEP ON KEEPIN ON!"; THE SMITHS "STILL ILL"; WORLD DOMINATION ENTERPRISES "ASBESTOS LEAD ASBESTOS"; THE MEKONS "DARKNESS AND DOUBT" (1984-85)

During the 1983 general election, while still a student, I did some canvassing for the Labour Party: a door-to-door, unswayable-voter-to-unswayable-voter trudge so discouraging that it permanently soured me on the frontline grunt-work that's the dreary, but indispensable, essence of political involvement. In the years between Labour's resounding defeat and the next election in 1987, a cluster of prominent left-wing musicians—Billy Bragg; Paul Weller, now fronting The Style Council; Jimmy Somerville of the Communards—formed an organization to mobilize the youth vote: Red Wedge. That name made aesthetes like me recoil. (Although the phrase's provenance turned out to be supercool—the title of a 1919 propaganda poster by Soviet modernist El Lissitzky—it probably sounded a lot better in Russian.) Me and my kind were also turned off by the overall aura of well-meaning worthiness that clung to the Red Wedge project, and the demeaning use of music as a mere vehicle. But by this point—I was now someone expressing beliefs and opinions publicly, writing for the UK weekly paper *Melody Maker*—I had become persuaded that politics in pop was a busted flush anyway. To me, the only artistically potent expressions of the political in late '80s music were expressions of impotence: the flailing rage of World Domination Enterprises; the dissident defiance of The Smiths; the despondency of the Mekons.

Despite Red Wedge's efforts, the 1987 election was another resounding defeat for Labour. This served to propel me even further into blissed-out anti-politics: The most adventurous music then being made, it seemed to me, hid from the world in gorgeous clouds of noise. Today, grown-up and worried, I feel retrospective sympathy for Red Wedge and the soul-influenced, militantly optimistic groups of that time—like The Redskins, who were aligned with the Socialist Workers Party rather than Labour. Why was I so down on the idea of preaching to the converted? When history is against them, the converted need to have their morale maintained, their spirits kept stalwart.

SPIRAL TRIBE
SOUND SYSTEM

FREE PARTY

TING POINT: STATION FISCHAMEND, 23.00

19.11.94

SPIRAL TRIBE
THE FREE FORCE OF TEKNO

SP 23   SP 23

SYSTEM ASSAULT SQUAD
TEKNO - TERRA - ATTACK
NEW VENUE + FREE + NONSTOP

TECHNOLOGY IS DESIGNING, BUILDING & MOVING INTO IT'S OWN FUTURE
FASTER THAN ANY OTHER SELF-GENERATING CIRCUIT.
WORD TRAVELS FAST THESE DAYS & MUSIC, THE UNSPOKEN WORD,
TRAVELS FASTER & LOUDER THAN EVER BEFORE.
THE EARTH IS RE - CONNECTED. THE SIGNAL IS READY TO BE SENT.

FULL ACADEMY LINE-UP AND MORE

23·1·93·INFO·081·959·752

THE EARTH IS RE - CONNECTED. THE SIGNAL IS READY TO BE SENT.

REDS STRIKE THE BLUES!
Ask not what parliament
can do for you
Do it yourself!

K.O! K.O!
Time & time when the workers rise, the
fightback's stabbed by a neat backstab &
the paper's lies. Leaders lead us into blind
retreat one by one we take the money ten by
ten we face defeat.

REDSKINS

REDS
STRIKE
THE BLUES

F1
0   7

REDSKINS: Nick King Chris Dean
Martin Hewes

THE REDSKINS BRASS
TRUMPET: Frank Burke
SAX: Lloyd Dwyer
TROMBONE: Nat Augustin

"K.O! K.O!" produced by Nick Lines for the Organization.
Recorded at the Roundhouse. REDS STRIKE THE
BLUES" produced by Johnny 'Guitar' Langford. Recorded
live at the Point.

FOR MORE INFORMATION CONTACT:
REDSKINS
P.O. BOX 45
MAN YO1 1XL

THE REINS IN OUR HANDS!
ORIGINATED BY GO DISCS FOR LONDON RECORDS
COVER: EM & M

RED WEDGE
it's time to
get BUSY
LABOUR LISTENS

UK POLITICS + POP

SPIRAL TRIBE AND RED WEDGE EPHEMERA COURTESY OF SIMON REYNOLDS

SPIRAL TRIBE "BREACH THE PEACE"; "FORWARD THE REVOLUTION" (1992)

It's May 1992 and, almost by chance, I've ended up at the largest public irruption of subcultural dissent the UK had seen since the concerts and rallies of the punk/Rock Against Racism era: Castlemorton, a mega-rave that takes over an area of unspoiled and secluded countryside in West England for a full seven days and draws crowds estimated at around 40,000. Castlemorton is "Anarchy in the U.K." for real, what '90s theoreticians call a "temporary autonomous zone": an instant city formed through the tribal alliance of urban ravers and post-hippie travelers who for decades have traversed the UK in caravans and trucks, visiting a summer circuit of free festivals.

I'm only there for the first night—by the time I get back to London, still blissed and babbling to anyone who'll listen, Castlemorton is a front-page story and the lead item on the TV news. Questions are asked in Parliament about what should be done to end the menace of nomadic ravers who could descend in hordes on any genteel village in the country, inflicting their noise and outlandish dress sense upon the powerless locals. Rumors abound of hairy, smelly travelers taking dumps in the front gardens of Castlemorton residents, or trying to sell drugs to local children.

Techno party crew Spiral Tribe, canny media operators and aspiring martyrs, take all the credit and all the blame. All 13 members are prosecuted for conspiracy to cause a public nuisance, in a long drawn-out case that would cost the public four million pounds, but end in acquittal. The truth is that there are no ringleaders behind Castlemorton: Its mass confluence was a viral happening, a swarming that anticipated the flash mobs of digital days and spiraled way larger than even its instigators had expected.

In the immediate aftermath of Castlemorton, while other sound systems shrewdly kept a low profile, Spiral Tribe do loads of interviews, talking about their aim to create a "public new sense," about how days and nights of non-stop drugged trance-dance could take you outside the limits of reality. The collective are given a record contract

from a label convinced they are techno's Sex Pistols. Actually, they're closer to Genesis P-Orridge's Psychic TV: literally a cult group, believers in conspiracy theories and magical-mystical forces, prophets for a new primitivism that has paradoxically been enabled by the do-it-yourself autonomy provided by digital technology.

In addition to the ultimately unsuccessful Spiral Tribe prosecution, the British government extends the clampdown on illegal raves with the Criminal Justice and Order Act of 1994, which vastly expands police powers to thwart rave organizers and to make life difficult for squatters and travelers. While the laws work their way through Parliament, their intended victims organize a protest movement, the Advance Party. This alliance of sound systems and civil liberties campaigners stages a couple of demonstrations in the summer and fall of 1994. The first, in July, is one of the few marches I've been on in my life. It winds up in Trafalgar Square, as is traditional for demos in the UK, but everything else about the protest—the garish, madcap clothes, the creatively designed placards—is wildly different from the drab norms of leftist activism.

I'm aware, though, with every step I take in the midst of this joyous cavalcade, that resistance is futile. Squatters, ravers, and travelers have few friends in the mainstream of British life: Ordinary folk are repelled by their appearance and talk, see them as parasitic layabouts, while figures of influence in politics and the media know that standing with "the crusties"—as they are popularly demonized—will do them no favors. The Criminal Justice Bill passes easily; Spiral Tribe splinters, with one faction moving to Europe to spread the "teknival" concept.

Like the Sex Pistols, Castlemorton proved once again the extraordinary power of music to upset and to disturb; how noise and words can shake reality, momentarily upturning common sense ideas of what's normal and proper and possible. But it also again showed the limitations of that power in the face of the forces that control the world. The idea of changing things through music is arguably a useful illusion, creating an urgent sense of mission and high stakes that again and again results in inspirational sounds and statements. But it could also be seen, more severely, as a diversion from the dirty, dreary work of struggle. ✎

VISUAL LIBERTY

We asked three visual artists to interpret what social justice could look like. Here's what they imagined.

On the opposite page, Los Angeles-based artist **CLEON PETERSON**, known for his monochromatic paintings of clashing figures, depicts the cruelty of humans. Next, on the following spread, London-based illustrator **LAURA CALLAGHAN**, with her flair for brightly colored detail and sharp-eyed editorial commentary, shows the rise of women.

Finally, London printmaker **GAURAB THAKALI** lends a contemplative image about Buffy Sainte-Marie, the Canadian music-tech innovator and activist for the rights of indigenous peoples and, indeed, all humans. These graphics have their own rhythms, their own tonal registers, their own music of liberation.

the SURV

a CONVERSATION
with M.I.A.

After using her art to open the world's eyes, M.I.A. has finally reached a sense
of peace. But that doesn't mean she's through speaking her mind.

BY ALEX FRANK

PHOTOGRAPHY MADS PERCH **STYLING** CARRI MUNDEN **HAIR** JAMES BROWN **MAKEUP** NINNI NUMMELA

M.I.A. *isn't*

DONE TALKING.

We are nearly an hour into a phone interview, the second of two, and her publicist beeps into the line, telling her that there are other calls to be made. But M.I.A. has something to say and, publicist be damned, she's going to say it. We had spent most of our time discussing her new album A.I.M.—a breezy jaunt of self-empowered odes to brushing off the haters, but then, through some invisible collaboration between two people as addicted to the language of controversy as everyone else in the world, our chat steers towards her most recent slew of contentious comments, the ones that got her dropped from this year's Afropunk festival in London. "It's interesting that in America the problem you're allowed to talk about is Black Lives Matter," she told a British newspaper in April. "Is Beyoncé or Kendrick Lamar going to say Muslim Lives Matter? Or Syrian Lives Matter? Or this kid in Pakistan matters? That's a more interesting question."

In the phone, she draws out every single languid syllable, attempting to explain her words in a way that would be more clear this time than it was before. And it is. Sort of. "I'm not going to get pushed into some corner for saying the truth," she tells me. "If people don't like it, they can fucking sit down. But I still stand by my view."

This is not the first time Maya Arulpragasam has had to defend herself, but if *A.I.M.* is any indication, it might be the last. Though the album's musical DNA is nearly retrospective in sound, adhering to and revitalizing the poppy electro rap that has long been her staple, for the first time in a while, she sounds like she's really having a good time. Her career has sometimes been overwhelmed by her penchant for acting outrageously, whether flipping off the cameras while performing with Madonna at the Super Bowl or continuously making comments about the Sri Lankan civil war that could seem careless, even though it's a subject dear to her heart as a refugee from the country. And, in recent years, her music has sounded bogged down, too. Her first two albums were incredibly promising templates for the future of global pop, including the radio-renewing smash "Paper Planes," but her middle period has been more scattered, from the aggressive distortions of her 2010 album *Maya* to the joyously perfect 2012 single "Bad Girls."

A.I.M. is less extreme on either end: It's something you could imagine putting on before a night out. A palate cleanser. When I tell her it's an album that makes me want a cocktail, she takes it as a compliment. Songs are called "Foreign Friend" and "Finally" and "Survivor," and she's assembled producers like Skrillex, Blaqstarr, and ex boyfriend/nemesis Diplo for beats. On album highlight "Freedun" there are even guest vocals by crooner heartthrob Zayn Malik, who helps her sing a saccharine (but totally effective) love song about stars shining and hearts beating. The first single and video, "Borders," is a bristling statement about the refugee crisis around the world, but throughout the rest of the album, the hooks are light, the beats are sparkling, and the swinging lyrics speak to tenacity and confidence and unbothered cool: "Dinosaurs died out and I'm still strong/A little bit of fun, yeah, I don't see it wrong."

Which is to say there's something of that original M.I.A. spark on here, the spark that made us all fall in love with a self-taught DIY artist who hustled her way through fashion college after living in a London council flat. She was the very first hipster pop star for a generation that has now created a space for many of them, from Robyn to Grimes to FKA twigs. She incorporated sounds from all over the world in a way that epitomized the internet's turn-of-the-century promise. She wore neon '80s hand-me-downs and bright British fashion when everyone else was still trying to look like the Strokes. She talked about immigration and social issues before "woke" was even a glimmer in the eyes of most musicians. Simply: For all her zigging and zagging, M.I.A. has been a massively consequential artist, and mostly we are better for it.

Calling from Mumbai, where she is filming a music video, she sounds inspired and relaxed. Even though the talk occasionally meanders into more pointed subjects, she sounds at peace with her life and her art and the world at large. In light of Donald Trump and Brexit and a refugee crisis that seems to have no end in sight, her newfound zen is surprising. But at 41, she has found a way forward, even if she still wanders off the trail from time to time.

77

TPR   **On this new record, you sound almost carefree, like you're finally having a lot of fun in your life and music. It's different from your last couple of albums, which were quite serious.**

M.I.A.   Am I carefree? Yeah. I'm not all serious. Damn. I am having fun. And it is about being human at the end of the day. You have to deal with yourself. The world is really crazy right now, and I feel like I've dealt with all that on my records: You can put *Arular* or *Kala* on and get the soundtrack to pretty much what is happening around the planet now. But after you get past [the craziness of the world], then you're going to need something to put on that connects to the basic human. If you forget all the political problems—not really forget, but understand—there has to be something beyond that. If you want to know what it feels like to be in the fight, you can listen to albums one or two. This album is just me actually accepting that life is just so bizarre.

There's parts that are even silly, like "Bird Song." Were you looking for a certain kind of musical looseness?

On this one, I wasn't like, "Oh my god, I have to go to the cutting-edge thing." I just wanted to go with what felt good on the day I was listening to it. It was very casual. I didn't want to make anything too electronic and EDM-y. And I just wanted to reference what I'd done before, and not really care about creating anything new. Just being comfortable with things you've created, and genres you've explored, instead of trying to run with it and be somewhere making some weird music, and somebody else comes along and makes a commercial song and then it becomes acceptable two years later. It was just about getting all these people together on the record.

There's a nice mixture of all races on there. There's black, white, and brown. This album just needs to be not a black thing, not a white thing, just the right thing. That's the slogan.

How did you go about writing lyrics for this album?

I'd go bop about and go to barbecues, hang out, go to a party or do something that made me really fucking happy, and then I'd write a song. When I was really happy, I'd be like, "I gotta go now." And then I'd be by myself for a couple hours and write a song and then come back to wherever I left.

You can hear that family reunion vibe on "Bird Song," especially the remix by Diplo, who you've feuded with pretty publically. How did you two patch things up?

There's a lot of water under the bridge, and if I can get on with him and he can get on with me after everything that has happened, that's a lot of hope for this world. He used to have dart boards with my face on it on his rider [*laughs*]. I was like, "I know that I should stab you, and you probably still want to stab me, but if we get on, that's actually quite a cool thing. And I just gotta believe in that thing. I don't want to take bitterness to the grave and hate you." And he's like that, too. It was 50-50. We're going to start from scratch. If I'm saying to people, "Yeah, everyone should tolerate each other," then I have to live by example. Rather than try to be a '90s rapper where I go, "Yeah, we're trying to kill each other," I have to show some way to get past that. Because life is so much bigger than that shit.

It's kind of funny to hear you sound so relaxed about life.

This is a weird one, this album. It's like

"IN ORDER for you to sell a lot of fucking records, you have to basically get rid of all the politics. At the end of the day, THAT IS THE CHOICE I HAD."

cleaning out your closet. And not having so much baggage.

Maybe you can relax because you finally feel accomplished: You have told the world to look at the refugee crisis your entire career, and now it's become a much more dominant mainstream political conversation.
My family said that to me. They were like, "The world has gone M.I.A." At one point, I was just not really ready to go back into the game. If your music was inspiring people to think and talk about it, and now it's being thought about and talked about, then it's like, "OK, you've done your job, you can walk away." But then I would have made this record to be the record you come to after you're done talking about it. Because after all that, some good comes out of it and some bad comes out of it. You still have to pick up the pieces and survive, whichever way the wind falls. I wanted to show that strength is pretty universal, and it's in everyone. My mind's been tested a lot, and some of that could have been because of my ignorance and it could have been my own doing. But most of it wasn't. Most of my fight was really [about] something that is out there.

Do you still believe that music can actually make a difference?
Yeah. When I see clever girls—girls who are smart and can do everything else and they're conscious—I think I contributed something to that.

I see a lof of your influence in FKA twigs and Grimes.
I love them as artists, but I feel like I almost want to protect them. I wouldn't want them to approach or talk about politics, because they do something to me aesthetically that makes me escape. And I think you need artists to serve that purpose. Actually, Michael Jackson is the ultimate entertainer in the world, but he was really political too. I don't know. Maybe we all have some sort of fragileness and outsiderness. Basically, it's tough to stand up to a lot of stuff unless you are actually coming from a lot of crazy shit.

A lot of people talk about how every time you came super close to a mainstream audience, you flipped off all of America at the Super Bowl or said something that you must've known would piss people off. But at this point, do you look back and think you self-sabotaged intentionally, even subconsciously? Did you not want fame?
That's not true. It's not about that. You do want to benefit people the most. The only thing I would say to that is that I could have shut up and put the glass slippers on and made millions of dollars. I could have made a ton of money and then helped build a school. But I wondered if that really worked. And at that time, I was like, *Can I sell?* Because in order for you to sell a lot of fucking records, you have to basically get rid of all the politics. At the end of the day, that is the choice I had. I'd come up talking about the refugee situation. And in 2009, I had a baby, and a month after my baby was born, they basically destroyed a lot of Tamil people in the space of two weeks in the Sri Lankan Civil War. It was really, really difficult to go through that. It's not really self-destruction. What the fuck do you do with the power after that? What do you do with the money after that? It just didn't make sense.

M.I.A.

In May, you tweeted that you don't have a visa to get into America. Are you still having troubles with that?

I don't know, you tell me. Can I hire you to investigate?

You've submitted an application and you can't get a response?

Yeah. I don't know what's happening with my visa. It'd be nice to meet Interscope and go and sit down and present the album. But it's a crazy time in America right now, which is why I can't really talk about what's happening in America on the album, because I'm not really there.

Before this interview, your publicist told me that you didn't want to discuss American politics.

I don't want to talk about America on this album because the only thing I have to offer is what somebody is thinking from outside. I'm not trying to have the same perspective as an American person from inside America. Because I'm not that. It's OK to have somebody who has a perspective from the outside. It was really interesting to say something and have everyone sort of turn on me and go, "Oh my god, you're the grossest human being." Because I was like, "No actually, from the outside, this is normal."

Are you speaking about your recent comments about Black Lives Matter—that American pop stars should speak up about the refugee crisis more?

When I said, "Oh, American artists can't say this and this and talk about global world issues." Sometimes my perspective doesn't relate to the one from inside America because I'm not there. I'm actually from the outside of America and I should be allowed to have that opinion and that dialogue. We do have different circumstances, different demographics, different experiences, different cultural things going on. I just felt like, at this point, it is important to listen to more perspectives around the world on this. Or just generally about anything.

So you were trying to say that we need American stars to stand up for the rights of refugees because there aren't Syrian ones who can?

Exactly. Because we're going to be waiting. It's annoying that I have to come out of retirement to tell you this. But that is the deal. This was my point: Either you expand yourself if you're going to represent the world, or let more people from the world come in and expand it for you. America is the person with the distribution platform and they are the ones that make icons on that level. When I open up my YouTube in India, in Scandinavia, in Bhutan, I'm going to get the same clips from the front page, which is American artists. They do have to step into where we are now. We're not in the '90s—we are now, and this is what's happening. Not everyone on earth sees the world from the American perspective. There are seven billion people on the planet that have their own experiences and ideas. And that's what I was saying, and everybody was only digesting me through their mirror and their view.

It's cool. In order to understand the real, you have to poke the situation. You might get into a scrap, you might have to take a few punches. But that's the only way you truly know the situation. America on the whole is a

83

privileged space for the rest of the world. And I think people forget that. From my perspective, when I see American artists, I think they are in a country where they can make that shit possible. They have the platform to do that. So if they wanted to raise awareness of something else in the world, they shouldn't shy away from it, because they are very much a part of all of these cases. And you can't deny that.

Let me approach it in another way, then: Since you've gotten so much heat in the past for things you've said, why not start parsing your words a little differently?
You know what, I'm satisfied with my fucking work. I'm interested in humanity and human beings. I want to do something positive. That is it. I don't care what fucking color you are. I don't care what fucking class you are. I don't care what geographical place you come from. I want to contribute to the present day. I think I've contributed. My work is born out of ideas coming together and people coming together and cultures coming together and colors coming together and music coming together. You have to tolerate that. That's the future. Being tolerant is the future. It's not being segregated.

But the world right now sometimes feels like it's moving in a more divided direction. Were you surprised by Brexit?
I'm surprised. Immigrants seem to be the hot topic and the very tool that's being used in order to create the division. And the whole immigrant refugee community is a really multi-faced, multi-faceted one. So right now, that image is being twisted because it's got a very specific face on it—"refugee" has a really specific picture to it right now. But it's not

specific. It's made up of so many different cultures and colors. Using that to create division is totally contradictory.

Why do you think all this xenophobia is fermenting right now?
I have no idea. But what's happening is massive. Human beings have to zoom out and look at the space on a much bigger level.

So are you worried?
Umm, nah.

How are you not worried about the state of the world right now?
Because you can't stop things from happening. You can't control it. That's one thing I can tell everyone. As the type of artist I am, and the ups and downs and the fights I've had in public, I never stand still and never accept that I've got to the destination and that this is it and now I'm going to put my feet up. I've never had that mentality. Evolution happens. It's inevitable. There's epic movement right now on the planet. It's really refreshing to me now that I can sit back and go, "Thank God. I was really honest about what I was." This is all I can do. I can honestly say from my life experience—even as an artist, even as a rapper, even as all these things—that I was constantly bombarding my head against loads of issues. I have gained all this knowledge through personal experience. I'm not getting this because it's a fad. I'm not doing it because it's a trend or because I heard somebody else say it. I'm telling you this is my personal experience. That shit fucking happens, but you fucking survive it if you want to fucking survive it. ✍

85

BLOOD & ECHOES:

THE STORY OF STEVE REICH'S CIVIL RIGHTS ERA MASTERPIECE

FIFTY YEARS AGO, THE COMPOSER DEBUTED HIS TAPE-LOOP EXPERIMENT *COME OUT*—A PIECE THAT PUT FORTH THE VOICE OF A MAN BEATEN BY POLICE, AN INJUSTICE THAT STILL REVERBERATES IN OUR BLACK LIVES MATTER MOMENT.

BY ANDY BETA   ILLLUSTRATIONS BY ARIEL DAVIS

ON A SPRING DAY IN 1964, POLICE IN HARLEM'S 32ND PRECINCT TRIED TO BEAT A CONFESSION OUT OF TWO BLACK TEENAGERS FOR A CRIME THEY DID NOT COMMIT. THE YOUNG MEN, WALLACE BAKER AND DANIEL HAMM, WERE REPEATEDLY BLUDGEONED WITH BILLY CLUBS WHILE IN CUSTODY, USING SUCH FORCE THAT THEY WERE TAKEN TO A NEARBY HOSPITAL FOR X-RAYS.

In an interview at the nearby Friendship Baptist Church a few days after the incident, the 18-year-old Hamm recounted being brutalized in shifts by six to 12 officers over the course of the night, along with the fact that "they got so tired beating us they just came in and started spitting on us." But even after hours of abuse, the cops wouldn't allow Hamm to be admitted for treatment, since he was not visibly bleeding. Thinking fast, Hamm reached down to one of the swollen knots on his legs where the blood had clotted beneath his skin: "I had to, like, open the bruise up, and let some of the bruise blood come out to show them."

Those 20 words, spoken by a young man who would unjustly remain in prison for nine years, still land like a truncheon. And utilizing just that one sentence, composer Steve Reich made one of the most visceral pieces of music of the 20th century. This year marks the 50th anniversary of *Come Out*, which made its live debut on April 17, 1966.

In a small way, the piece helped bring about justice for Hamm and other victims of police brutality. It also established the heretofore-unknown Reich as one of the most adventurous modern American composers and became a touchstone of avant-garde and electronic music. And now, with increased scrutiny brought to bear on police brutality in minority communities, the rise of the Black Lives Matter movement, and the vast American carceral state, Hamm's voice echoes through other names that have recently come into our consciousness: Trayvon Martin, Eric Garner, Michael Brown, Sandra Bland, Terence Crutcher. As looped by Reich, the phrase "come out to show them" anticipates powerful hashtags like #ICantBreathe and #SayHerName. For better and worse, the story of *Come Out*—its unlikely genesis and its aftermath—still resonates.

The incident that led to Hamm's bruises and blood began with the most innocent of acts: a capsized fruit cart, and a group of Harlem school children who threw the fallen grapefruits around like baseballs. But when the shop's owner whistled for them to stop, the sound alerted the local police, who reportedly descended upon the kids with a viciousness that frightened all passersby. It was then that Hamm and Baker stepped between the children and the cops, attempting to defuse the situation.

"I saw this policeman with his gun out and with his billy in his hand," Hamm recounted. "I like put myself in the way to keep him from shooting the kids. Because first of all he was shaking like a leaf and jumping all over the place. And I thought he might shoot one of them."

In James Baldwin's 1966 essay "A Report from Occupied Territory," written as a response to the incidents of that day and the subsequent travesty of justice that followed, he likened his home of Harlem to a police state. "The police are simply the hired enemies of this population," he wrote. "They are present to keep the Negro in his place and to protect white business interests, and they have no other function." Even in the face of something as innocent as bruised fruit and kids being kids, the fact remains: "Occupied territory is occupied territory... and it is axiomatic... that any act of resistance, even though it be executed by a child, be answered at once, and with the full weight of the occupying forces." Hamm and Baker were arrested, despite the shop owner's admission that the teens were not involved in the incident.

And while Hamm's bloodletting did allow him to get medical attention and be released, his freedom was short-lived. Ten days later, on April 30, the stabbing death of Margit Sugar at her used-clothing store in Harlem brought the police back to the teenager's door. Along with Hamm, they rounded up five other teens: Baker, Walter Thomas, William Craig, Ronald Felder, and Robert Rice. Despite a paucity of evidence and the prosecution's star witness being the one most likely to have actually committed the crime, this group—deemed the "Harlem Six"—was charged with murder, for which the penalty in New York State was death by electric chair. Hamm and the others would remain incarcerated for the next nine years.

89

"No one in Harlem will ever believe that the Harlem Six are guilty," Baldwin wrote of the imprisoned teens and the court process that disallowed them from having their own counsel. Soon, the news media distorted their case even further, with the *New York Times* portraying the Six as members of an anti-white gang called the Blood Brothers. The NAACP insisted that no civil liberties had been violated in the case, but as summer progressed, another instance of police violence—the shooting death of James Powell, a 15-year-old black boy—led to roiling riots in Harlem and Brooklyn's Bedford-Stuyvesant neighborhood, precipitating further unrest in Philadelphia, Chicago, Rochester, and throughout New Jersey. Over the next four years, race riots would rage from Watts in Los Angeles, to Detroit and Washington, D.C.

Eventually, the plight of the imprisoned Harlem Six came to the attention of civil rights activist Truman Nelson, as well as a number of celebrities: Baldwin and actor Ossie Davis, poets Amiri Baraka and Allen Ginsberg, philosopher Bertrand Russell, and John Lennon and Yoko Ono. Nelson recorded interviews with the boys and their mothers and put them together into a book entitled *The Torture of Mothers* in order to raise awareness about their case. In an effort to raise money to cover legal fees for a retrial, Nelson set about organizing a benefit concert in 1966. In addition to protest songs and speeches from supporters, Nelson wanted to have his interview tapes edited to tell the story of the Harlem Six.

"I got a call from Truman Nelson saying: 'I heard that you work with tape,'" Steve Reich, now 80, tells me over the phone 50 years later. "I thought, I'm not a tape editor, but yeah, I've worked with it." Reich had realized his first tape piece the year before, based on a recording he made of San Francisco Pentecostal street preacher Brother Walter talking about Noah and the great flood. Walter proclaimed: "It's gonna rain."

Reich imagined that line as being sung in rounds and made two tape loops to test out his theory. But as he pressed play on his tape machines, a funny thing happened: The loops began in synch and then, as Reich recalls, "ever so gradually, the sound moved over my left ear and then down my left side and then slithered across the floor and began to reverberate and really echo. That whole process immediately struck me as a complete, seamless, uninterrupted way of making a piece that I had never anticipated." Rather than a round about the rain, the sound turned apocalyptic. *It's Gonna Rain* became Reich's first major composition.

By 1966, Reich had returned to his home of New York City and was situated in a studio downtown when he first met Nelson. At that point, Reich was unfamiliar with the trial and events surrounding the Harlem Six. The burgeoning Civil Rights Movement was one of the biggest concerns of the day, yet Reich in some way felt on the outside of the situation. "I wasn't doing anything about it really," he admits. But he agreed to edit together Nelson's 20 hours of analog interview tapes into a coherent narrative pro bono, under one condition: permission to make a piece along the same lines of *It's Gonna Rain* if he found the right phrase. Nelson agreed.

The composer says he was looking "to find the key phrase, the exact wording of which would sum up the whole situation... and the tone of Hamm's voice, the speech melody, and what he says encapsulated a lot of what was going on in the civil rights movement at that time." Reich hums the line's cadence over the phone. "When I heard that, I thought, This is going to make a really, really, really interesting piece."

The composition opens with Hamm's statement repeated three times before the two tape loops begin to move out of phase with each other. That subtle shift at first gives Hamm's voice a slight echo and, by the three-minute mark, the words are swathed in reverb as the voices move out of sync. As the loops build, Hamm's concrete imagery transforms into something hazy and unrecognizable as speech. As writer Linda Winer once put it in describing

Reich's tape works: "At first you hear the sense of the words—a common statement with cosmic vengeance inside. Then, like with any word repetition, the sounds become nonsense… And one is transfixed in a bizarre combination of the spiritual and the mechanistic."

For all of its subsequent influence, *Come Out* had an inconspicuous, even subliminal debut that April night at Manhattan's Town Hall. The benefit, hosted by the Charter Group for the Harlem Six, featured protest songs, dramatizations from *The Torture of Mothers*, Reich's commissioned audio narrative, and a speech by Ossie Davis, who had delivered the eulogy for Malcolm X the year before. Attendees would be hard-pressed to recall *Come Out*, though, and it received no notice or reviews in the press.

"The world premiere of *Come Out* was as pass-the-hat music," Reich says with a laugh. Was there a reaction from the crowd? "Yeah, people were reaching in their pockets! I don't think people paid a great deal of attention to the music. They just thought it was some kind of funny sound effect that was atmospheric to get them to contribute. It wasn't a concert situation at all!"

Funds raised at the event allowed the Harlem Six and their families to pay for civil rights lawyer Conrad Lynn and other legal fees. Their case went to appeal in 1968, but retrials and three hung juries stretched the proceedings to 1973. After being held without bail for nine years, they finally plead to manslaughter in exchange for suspended sentences. Daniel Hamm was released the following year and has since avoided the public record. (I managed to get in contact with Hamm, who is now 70 years old, but he declined to comment for this story.) While a touchstone in the fight for civil rights, the case of the Harlem Six has almost vanished from popular culture as well. But *Come Out* continues to loop. In a 2009 essay, music academic Sumanth Gopinath wrote: "In retrospect, [*Come Out*] served as the most prominent historical memorial for the legal and political drama known as the Harlem Six case."

The month after *Come Out*'s low-key premiere, Reich performed at the Park Place Gallery in SoHo, a venue where his tape pieces were presented so that they closely aligned with minimalist art and sculpture. The show was reviewed in the Village Voice, which cited *Come Out* and noted: "Mr. Reich's strident, reiterative work… suggested a raga exercise, distorting and distorting to incandescence." In 1967, *Come Out* was recorded and released on CBS-Odyssey's "Music of Our Time" record series, alongside titans of modern composition including John Cage, Karlheinz Stockhausen, Pierre Boulez, Morton Feldman, and Terry Riley. It announced Reich's arrival and garnered positive reviews in *Time* and *New York* magazine.

By the time of Hamm was released from prison in 1974, Reich was at the vanguard of new American composition. Almost exactly 10 years after *Come Out* made its debut, he returned to Town Hall to present the world premiere of his landmark work, *Music for 18 Musicians*. "*Come Out* was the end of my working with tape, but it was the start of my taking the principle of phasing discovered with it and applying it to live musicians," Reich says. "It was the beginning of a highway, really, to the music of the rest of my life… the end of something and the beginning of something, simultaneously."

In the mid-'60s, electronic music was beginning to venture out from academia into popular music and culture, thanks to early adopters ranging from the BBC Radiophonic Workshop to Wendy Carlos' *Switched-On Bach* to the Beatles citing Karlheinz Stockhausen as an influence. But compositions like these required room-sized computers, expensive prototypes or rare synthesizers to enact. When it was released alongside such technologically rigorous compositions on that 1967 compilation album, *New Sounds in Electronic Music*, Reich's *Come Out* stood out. The other works utilized sine wave generators and oscilloscopes, drawing on the resources at larger academic institutions, whereas *Come Out* was deceptively simple, the sound of the human voice captured on tape in an unadorned, documentary manner. Its implication was clear: Anyone with a tape recorder might be able to find new sounds in older ones.

Made in an era of mind-altering music and electronic effects, *Come Out* stands as psychedelic in its purest sense, finding something hallucinatory in the most ba-

AS THE CONCRETE DETAILS OF HAMM'S

BEATING WERE SLOWLY ERASED AMID YEARS

OF TRIALS AND NEW RACIAL ATROCITIES

PERPETUATED BY LAW ENFORCEMENT, COME

OUT EVEN ANTICIPATES THE SORT OF NUMBNESS

AND EXHAUSTION THAT NOW RESULTS FROM

A 24/7 NEWS CYCLE THAT BLENDS OUTRAGES

AND ATROCITIES INTO A DANGEROUS,

UNDIFFERENTIATED MASS.

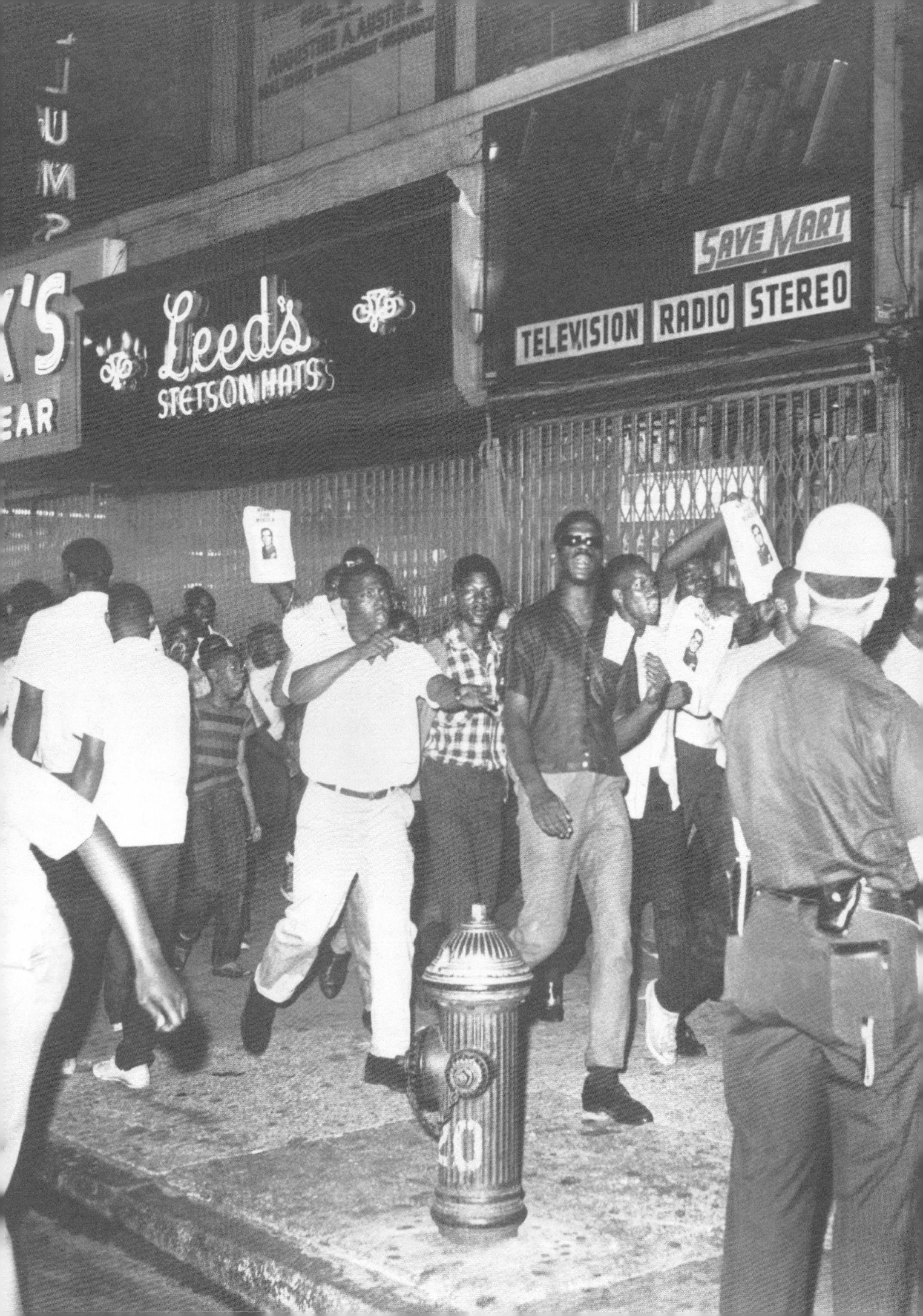
Leed's
STETSON HATS
SAVE MART
TELEVISION
RADIO
STEREO

sic of instruments. From these simple means an entire bewildering world of sound emerge, and the connotations of this transformation are vast.

Different listeners have heard larger metaphors in the composition: from urban uprisings and rioting, to the duplicity of voices signifying schizophrenia, to a Kafkaesque grinding up of Hamm in the machinations of bureaucracy and the justice system. There is something psychotic that bubbles up throughout the piece—a brutality and horror in the disaffection of Hamm's speaking voice, in the image of bruise blood being squeezed so as to break the surface of his own skin, in a self-mutilation that reveals a greater injury. As the concrete details of Hamm's beating were slowly erased amid years of trials and new racial atrocities perpetuated by law enforcement, Come Out even anticipates the sort of numbness and exhaustion that now results from a 24/7 news cycle that blends outrages and atrocities into a dangerous, undifferentiated mass.

And just as the piece has been interpreted intellectually, it's rang out through various artistic environments as well. Captain Beefheart bellowed the central phrase multiple times on 1969's Trout Mask Replica. And in 1982, it provided the soundtrack for Fase, a dance piece by Belgian choreographer Anne Teresa De Keersmaeker, Michèle Anne De Mey, and Jennifer Everhard that is now considered a cornerstone of contemporary dance.

But Come Out's lasting artistic influence is most deeply felt in electronic music and DJ circles, factoring into ambient, house, trance, and trip-hop, and utilized by the likes of Orbital, UNKLE, and D*Note. Madlib cut up Hamm's voice for the Madvillainy single "America's Most Blunted." Come Out opened Leon Vynehall's recent BBC Radio 1's Essential Mix and it lies at the heart of Nicolas Jaar's Resident Advisor 500 Mix. Though musical references to Come Out often focus on its trance-inducing texture rather than its message, Jaar's usage reengages with the piece's history. Not five minutes earlier in his mix, Jaar samples a line from dub poet Linton Kwesi Johnson about "when the present is haunted by the past," and then Daniel Hamm's voice and blood come out in response. It's a strange moment, with the brutality of the line haunting a sumptuous modern beat.

Reich says that because of the threat of mutual nuclear annihilation, begat by the Cuban Missile Crisis in 1962, It's Gonna Rain is "about the destruction of the world." And, with Come Out, he wanted to do a piece that was as emotionally charged, "which is based in the real world around you." Documentary material has shaped Reich's oeuvre ever since, all the way through 2011's WTC 9/11, which incorporates voice recordings that surrounded the September 11 attacks. "I'm documenting reality to portray something honestly without understatement or overstatement," he says. "The key has been to stick to the facts."

Was Come Out made as a piece of agitprop? "I think a lot of 'political pieces' are, to put it kindly, a waste of time," Reich says. "If it's a really good piece of music, then the political purpose to which it's put is betrayed by the sense in which music will just vaporize, and the theme will vaporize along with it." So while it might never be a rallying cry for a crowd of protesters, Come Out played a part in the Civil Rights Movement, and each ensuing sample of it acknowledges the history and struggle that led to its creation.

For his part, Reich offers up another work of art as a parallel: Pablo Picasso's 1937 mural, Guernica. It's one of Picasso's most famous pieces, a massive, grotesque gray painting measuring more than 11 feet tall and 25 feet wide. It's one of the most recognizable artworks of the 20th century, inspired by the report of a bombing of a Basque village in Spain on April 26, 1937. "It was deliberate civilian bombing for the first time," Reich says. "What has become commonplace, the very nature of terrorism in our day—which is to aim for civilians—had never happened until Guernica." In painting Guernica, Picasso brought worldwide attention to the horrors of the Spanish Civil War, its name and imagery lasting even if the event behind it is no longer known. "Because it is such an outstanding painting, [it] has kept the memory of this town, and the significance of this bombing as a kind of memorial," Reich says. "Good art preserves the stuff it's about." ✒

95

LEGENDARY:

Gerard Gaskin has spent more than two decades photographing the house ballroom scene in New York, Washington, D.C., Richmond, Va., and Philadelphia. Gaskin's 2013 book *Legendary: Inside the House Ballroom Scene* captures the intimate radiance of a scene born, as he has written, "out of a need for black and Latino gays to have a safe space to express themselves." He documented these late-night pageants in their onstage exuberance and their backstage grace from the close perspective of someone who has immersed himself in the culture, which has grown more fluid, open, and accessible since he began observing it, when the AIDS epidemic was at its tragic nadir. The following images are culled from the book, as well as Gaskin's personal archive.

PHOTOGRAPHS BY GERARD GASKIN

PREVIOUS PAGE: BABY GARCON WALKING WOMAN'S RUNWAY AT THE TONY, ANDREA AND ERIC BALL, 2000. YWCA, 3RD AVENUE & ATLANTIC AVENUE, BROOKLYN, NY.
THIS PAGE: JLIN EVISU GETTING READY FOR THE BALENCIAGA BALL, 2005. WASHINGTON, D.C.

STEWART EBONY WALKING TALL BOY BUTCH QUEEN RUNWAY, STATE TO STATE BALL, 1998. YMCA, 135TH STREET AND ADAM CLAYTON POWELL BLVD. HARLEM, NY.

DOMINIQUE AND BEVERLY BACKSTAGE AT THE EVISU BALL, 2006. NATIONAL BLACK THEATRE, 126TH STREET AND 5TH AVENUE HARLEM, NY.

THIS PAGE: JAY BLAHNIK BALL, 2001. PHILADELPHIA, PA. | FACING PAGE: GERALD LA BEIJA BACKSTAGE AT THE PRADA BALL, PREPARING TO WALK
THE BUTCH QUEEN RUNWAY, 1999. THE HOWARD JOHNSON HOTEL, 57TH STREET AND 10TH AVENUE, MANHATTAN, NY.

SINIA EBONY AT THE PARIS DUPREE BALL, 2000. BEFORE THE BALL STARTS, THEY INTRODUCE LEGENDS, STATEMENTS AND STARS; THEY CALLED SINIA OUT TO VOGUE. YWCA, 3RD AVENUE AND ATLANTIC AVENUE, BROOKLYN, NY.

BACKSTAGE, LATEX BALL, 2005. THE MANHATTAN CENTER, 34TH STREET AND 8TH AVENUE, MANHATTAN, NY.

SINIA EBONY AND THE HOUSE OF
EBONY AT LAB NIGHTCLUB, 2002.
BROOKLYN, NY.

THIS PAGE: STATE TO STATE BALL, 1998. YMCA, 135TH STREET AND ADAM CLAYTON POWELL BLVD, HARLEM, NY. | FACING PAGE: CHARLY AND MATHYAS, EBONY BALL, 1997. THE MARC BALLROOM UNDER THE COFFEE SHOP RESTAURANT, 16TH STREET AND UNION SQUARE, MANHATTAN, NY.

DANIELLE REVLON GOING TO A YEAR-
END BALL, 1997. BROOKLYN, NY.

THE LEGENDS BALL, 1997. THE MARC BALLROOM UNDER THE COFFEE SHOP RESTAURANT, 16TH STREET AND UNION SQUARE, MANHATTAN, NY.

DERAY MCKESSON ON THE POWER OF PROTEST MUSIC

THE BLACK LIVES MATTER ACTIVIST DISCUSSES HOW THE WORK OF ARTISTS LIKE KENDRICK, BEYONCÉ, AND D'ANGELO PLAYS A CRUCIAL ROLE IN KEEPING THE MOVEMENT MOVING.

BY MARC HOGAN

activist DeRay Mckesson isn't a musician, but he knows how powerful the right song can be in the fight for justice. "Music helps shape the way people think about the world and act in the world," he says. He's seen that influence firsthand: In August 2014, he took a leave of absence from his job as a Minneapolis public school administrator to go protest the shooting death of Michael Brown by police in Ferguson, Missouri. Mckesson's unsparing on-the-ground Twitter commentary quickly vaulted him to national prominence.

Of course, the Civil Rights Movement in the 1960s also had its protest anthems, like "We Shall Overcome," along with motivational hits by stars like Sam Cooke and Curtis Mayfield. And much as civil rights icons like Rep. John Lewis of Georgia went from demonstrating to passing laws, Mckesson finds himself at a similar crossroads. This year, he made the leap from activism to politics by running for mayor in his hometown of Baltimore, though he was defeated in the Democratic primary.

But like this movement's music, which has grown more and more political from figures as lofty as Kendrick Lamar and Beyoncé, Mckesson hasn't stopped. In June, the 31-year-old went to work for the Baltimore public school district. The following month, he was arrested while demonstrating in Baton Rouge, Louisiana, and as of press time his lawsuit against that city over his treatment is still ongoing. He also remains a vocal and influential presence on social media, where he continues to advocate for racial equality.

Reached immediately after he visited Washington, D.C.'s new National Museum of African American History and Culture, Mckesson talked with TPR about the music of modern activism, what it means to be an ally, and the stakes of the 2016 presidential election.

TPR **What's the role of music in Black Lives Matter and modern activism?**

DERAY MCKESSON We didn't invent resistance or discover injustice in August of 2014. We exist in a legacy of struggle. And through all of it, music has played an important role, whether we think about the old Negro spirituals, or the birth of hip-hop and rap, or today's chants in the street. Whether it's through Kendrick's song ["Alright"], or Beyoncé's album *Lemonade*, music continues to be a way that we both process the world that we live in today and imagine what is possible.

Why is it so powerful when artists like Kendrick and Beyoncé speak out about these issues in their music?
We aren't born woke. Something wakes us up. For some people, that's a video of police violence, or their proximity to a friend, or a protest. For some people it's art. There are many ways that people begin to understand the world better and deeper, and music is one of those ways.

Especially in blackness, liberation music has been key to our understanding of the current state and has helped imbue a sense of hope even in the most trying times. Kendrick's "Alright" does that—it acknowledges the trauma and says we'll be OK. And *Lemonade* is one way that Beyoncé has used her public platform to express her love and appreciation for blackness, specifically as a black woman.

Beyond your Kendricks and Beyoncés, what other artists do you think are making work that really matters now?
I thought D'Angelo's last album [2014's *Black Messiah*] was a liberation album. It deeply talked about what it meant to be vulnerable, to be black, to be a man, to be a partner, and it came out in a context of unrest, which is important to remember. The line "I will never betray my heart" [from the *Black Messiah* song "Betray My Heart"] is in my profile on Twitter.

And I remember there was a lot of Lil Boosie playing at the protests in August and September of 2014, along with a lot of people making and remixing chants.

What do you feel you accomplished with your run for mayor of Baltimore?
We have to be as organized on the inside as we are on the outside. That has to be part of the strategy. I haven't written about the election yet, but it was so powerful to connect with the voters every day. And it was a short campaign: If I would do anything differently, it would have been to start earlier.

But it was powerful to connect with people who believe in a different type of possibility in the city and use technology to do that. After that, I became the interim chief of human capital for Baltimore City Public Schools. So I'm there for now. My career after college was education. I was a teacher, I worked in an after-school program, I trained teachers. I've returned to that work because I believe in the new superintendent and I believe in kids.

What do people outside Baltimore need to know about what's going on there these days?
The problems are at scale, and the solutions need to be. There's a lot of promise in the city, but, like in so many cities, we have to start thinking about how to marshal resources to be at scale.

How are all these social issues affecting the culture and the music in Baltimore?
The arts scene in Baltimore is really rich and very vibrant. It's one of the untold stories of the city.

Trauma takes away people's power, and part of our collective work is to help people reclaim their power at the individual level and restore power at the system level. Art and music has a role to play in that. I think about so many people for whom music is one of the ways that they process the world, the way they've understood their own gifts, the way they've relearned or learned anew how to believe in themselves, or how they've been exposed to new ideas and new perspectives. In liberation work, it's a conversation about how we process the world to make it better.

117

"WE AREN'T BORN WOKE. SOMETHING WAKES US UP. THERE ARE MANY WAYS THAT PEOPLE BEGIN TO UNDERSTAND THE WORLD BETTER AND DEEPER, AND MUSIC IS ONE OF THOSE WAYS."

What role can white allies play, and at the same time, what shouldn't white people do?

Part of the work moving forward is building a coalition that leverages our collective power to make an impact and effect serious change. White people have a role to play in that. It requires the white people to understand that they are to use their privilege to disrupt injustice, that it is about asking people what they need. It is not about telling people what they're supposed to do and how they're supposed to fight for liberation. I've seen well-intentioned white people say, "This is what you need to do to get free." That is not what it means to be an ally. It means you can use your resources, access, and skills to assist people as they ask for it. To partner with people.

I just saw someone tweet about a black woman who got pulled over by police, and how a bystander stopped and used her privilege as a white woman to engage in watching the police officer. She knew that her whiteness provided a different level of protection in that moment, which she leveraged. That's what it means to be an ally.

What do you think is at stake with this upcoming presidential election?

In general, all of this is a question of: Can we organize? No matter who the next president is, black people need to be organized. We need to continue to innovate in the way that we think about leveraging the collective power of black people.

Trump is dangerous. This is not an election about the lesser of two evils. There is one clear evil. There is another candidate that people have real concerns about. And if Trump is president, I think that his administration will do real structural damage that will take years or decades for us to undo.

How does your identity as a gay man inform your politics?

The goal is that we live in a world where people don't experience injustice, and the movement has been focused on making sure that it's true across identities. I'm a black, gay man, and I should be able to live in a world where I'm able to live in the complexity of my identity in a way that is safe and secure, like everyone else.

It's important to me to talk about the fullness of my identity, because I'm in it. I also know that people experience my blackness before they experience my sexuality. If you don't know anything about me, you just see me and you see my blackness. But I experience my full identity as full each time, even though other people might not.

It's important that people fight for and build a world that is not racist, that is not homophobic, that is not sexist. But we have to fight across all of those intersections. We can do that and not lose focus on race. This is not an either-or. This is a both-and.

What are your thoughts about social media as a tool? You have used it for justice, but then somebody like Donald Trump has also harnessed its power. Is it a double-edged sword?

We're at the beginning of seeing the power of social media. The landscape of what is news and who gets to tell their story to the public is suddenly changing, and social media is fueling that change. The reality is that there are people with wildly varying perspectives on the world, and everybody has the potential to become a storyteller, whether the stories are dangerous, damaging, and bigoted, or whether they're productive and powerful. People continue to manage how those conversations rise to the top better and better.

Donald Trump is only dangerous because people are listening. As the way the crowd interacts becomes more sophisticated, I'm hopeful that we'll see the bigoted, sexist, and racist messages overcome by a crowd that is healthy and accepting. I think about how there's a community on Black Twitter that continues to refine over and over—how it shifts, moves, and responds to trauma and joy.

What's next for you?

I'm interested in continuing to build out ways of organizing that allow as many people that want to be part of it as possible, and that doesn't require or pretend that chapters and members are the only way to organize people. The next part of the work is to get a critical mass of people with the skills to keep thinking about it and move in tandem. I'm excited about that. ✎

119

GOD IS ON THE LOOSE!

BY ANDY BETA

Draped in lime green and black plastic, choked by necklaces made of electrical cords and alligator teeth, Caetano Veloso was ready for the Festival International de Canção (International Song Festival), a year-old original-song competition meant to foster cultural exchange. It was Sept. 15, 1968 and the singer and his backing band Os Mutantes—looking and sounding like they had just crashed to planet Earth—were set to perform before a boisterous crowd of students. But "É Proibido Proibir" ("Prohibiting is Prohibited") was no ordinary song, it was a pop provocation inspired by the May '68 riots in Paris. Opening with atonal noise, Veloso had his sights on the conservative student audience as he began to sway his hips provocatively. As he wrote in his 1997 memoir *Tropical Truth*, "The hatred... on the faces of the spectators was fiercer than I could have imagined." As the strange new song started, the crowd turned their backs on the band.

Veloso's friend and close ally Gilberto Gil had already been booed and instantly disqualified from the contest for his Jimi Hendrix-inspired new single "Questão de Ordem" ("Points of Order"), yet Veloso brought him onstage to protest the festival, its audience, and the future of Brazil itself. As you can hear on "Ambiente De Festival," a live recording of this moment (and the B-side to "Proibido"), the performance was as raw as any punk single, the audience's roar a terrifying din. In turn, Veloso launched an invective at the crowd: "So, you're the young people who say they want to take power! If you're the same in politics as you are in music, we're done for! Disqualify me with Gil. The jury is very nice, but incompetent. God is on the loose!" The musicians were then pelted with cups, fruit, eggs, and chunks of wood. As they left the theater to screams, they worried at what other forces had shaken loose that night.

Tropicália was a movement that lasted just short of a year, spanning from artist Hélio Oiticica's 1967 art installation of the same name (wherein viewers walked along a tropical sand path only to come face-to-face with a television set) to the debut of a television show wherein its constituents buried the movement on-air. But Tropicália's influence was vast. A loose collective that included Veloso, Gil, Os Mutantes, vocalist Gal Costa, songwriter-composer Tom Zé, bossa nova singer Nara Leão, Brazilian-pop performer Jorge Ben, arranger Rogério Duprat—along with visual artists, experimental poets, playwrights, and filmmakers—these creatives modernized Brazilian culture just as the country's ruling military junta began to strangle democracy and expression. Tropicália produced only a handful of albums and a compilation, but it went on to transform Música Popular Brasileira (MPB) and future generations from Brazil and around the world. As author Christopher Dunn put it in *Brutality Garden*, his 2001 book on the movement, this was "simultaneously an exciting period of countercultural experimentation and severe political repression."

The '60s were a fraught time for Brazil and the Tropicalistas struck a precarious balance between political extremes. In 1962, Brazilian president João Goulart took office and attempted to move his country to the left with a series of reforms. By April Fool's Day, 1964, a CIA-assisted military coup d'état toppled his administration and moved the country to the far right. In this climate, artists had to walk a thin line between the communist left and the increasingly prohibitive military regime on the right. On one side, students and intellectuals protested that their art and music was insufficiently political, crassly embracing American pop culture instead of Brazilian music, while the other side was concerned they weren't nationalist enough. Imbibing the heady works of Bob Dylan, Jean-Luc Godard,

TROPICÁLIA DIDN'T CONQUER THE DICTATORSHIP,

Pink Floyd, Luis Buñuel—as well as taking in the revolts in France and the rise of the Black Power movement in the U.S.—the Tropicalistas amalgamated the countercultural trends of the decade and brought them to bear on their own heritage. Gilberto Gil's 1968 ritualistic rocker "Bat Macumba" succinctly contains the collective's concerns: It evokes Bahian religious cults macumba and candomblé, as well as Batman. Written out, the lyrics reveal their concrete poetry roots, as the words even look like bat wings.

"The idea of cultural cannibalism fit tropicalistas like a glove; we were 'eating' the Beatles and Jimi Hendrix," Veloso later said. "We wanted to participate in the worldwide language both to strengthen ourselves as a people and to affirm our originality." In the lineage of 20th century Brazilian music, Tropicália intermingled with outside sounds in much the same ways as its predecessors had: Samba took in Argentinean tangos and American foxtrot; bossa nova dug west coast jazz; and Jovem Guarda was the sound of American rock'n'roll. Tropicalistas chewed the blotter of '60s psychedelia and brought these kaleidoscopic visions to bear on their love for colorful film star Carmen Miranda, the drunken drums of Carnival, and underpinning it all, João Gilberto's bossa nova.

Tropicália took root in the oppressive shadow of the junta. Naomi Klein's *The Shock Doctrine* describes disposed president Goulart as "an economic nationalist committed to land redistribution, higher salaries, and a daring plan to force foreign multinationals to reinvest a percentage of their profits back into the Brazilian economy"—three notions that sought to bridge the gap between rich and poor. It was a plan decidedly at odds with the American government and economist Milton Friedman's influential theories, which instead touted deregulation, hyper-inflation, the privatization and outsourcing of a country's natural resources to multinational corporations, plus cutbacks on all social programs. From the mid-'60s into the '90s, throughout the Southern Cone, the brutal, CIA-approved, corporation-funded, U.S.-friendly regimes of General Augusto Pinochet in Chile, Jorge Videla in Argentina, and President Artur da Costa e Silva in Brazil were in firm control and Friedman's caustic theories were mercilessly put into practice. Hundreds of thousands of deaths and

"disappearances" followed those who opposed such measures throughout South America—be they union leaders, academics, or students.

But according to Klein, President Costa e Silva almost made a tactical error, imposing these punitive measures in half-steps: "There were no obvious shows of brutality, no mass arrests... the junta also made a point of keeping some remnants of democracy in place, including limited press freedoms and freedom of assembly. By 1968 the streets were overrun with anti-junta marches... and the regime was in serious jeopardy."

At first, the military's measures didn't overtly affect Tropicália—the movement's inherent playfulness allowed artists to elude censors with urbane pop-cultural references and to comment slyly on the state of affairs. Tropicália's incisiveness might be best summed up in the title of Tom Zé's "Catechism, Toothpaste and Me," where the newly instilled consumer capitalism replaces Catholicism in the minds of middle-class Brazil. An early Veloso love song replaces the moon with the glow of an Esso gas station sign, seemingly embracing the American multinational petroleum giant, yet also winking at how increased consumerism has altered the landscape in the wake of the coup.

And then there's Os Mutantes' "Panis Et Circencis" ("Bread and Circuses"). It was both the band's dizzying debut and the subtitle of the epochal Tropicália compilation album, which featured Veloso, Gil, Costa, and Zé—and served as a loose group manifesto, the *Sgt. Pepper's* of Brazil. "Panis" took the title from Roman poet Juvenal's line about the means of appeasement for mass culture (perfect for a three-minute pop song). Even if you don't speak Portuguese, it's a stunning sonic confection: triumphant horn fanfare, dreamy

THOUGH IT PROVIDED HOPE AND LIGHT IN BRAZIL'S DARKEST YEARS.

123

vocal pop that turns into a psychedelic fuzz bomb. Midway through, the song suddenly melts like film stuck in a projector, ending in a chaotic din of silverware, musique concrete noise, and Strauss' "The Blue Danube Waltz." But under that racket lies Rita Lee's pointed critique of the bourgeoisie class, complacent during the coup: "I tried to sing/My illuminated song... but the people in the dining room are busy being born and dying."

Even amid the whimsy of the Tropicalistas, the local air of violence began to creep into their lyrics. Gil's "Miserere Nóbis" tucks in references to stains of wine and blood and ends with gunshots and booming cannons. Dulcet bossa nova singer Gal Costa, later an adult contemporary MPB superstar, grew wilder and more psychedelic, roaring out a warning on "Divino Maravilhoso" ("Divine, Wonderful") about paying attention to the blood on the ground. (Her 1969 album *Gal* is the equivalent of Barbra Streisand recording with Boredoms and remains one of the heaviest documents of Tropicália).

As 1968 dragged on, the situation in Brazil worsened. Industrial strikes and student marches became frequent and armed guerrilla groups formed in the jungles. Veloso, Gil, and other well-known Brazilian singers, actors, and authors participated in Passeata dos cem mil (March of One Hundred Thousand) in Rio, which the police violently crushed. The climate turned increasingly fraught as the military struggled to keep control. Death squads began to prowl the streets and, as noted in *Brasil: Nunca Mais*—a report published in 1985 that reckoned with the dictatorship's torture record—extralegal police forces renowned for their sadism also appeared, funded "by contributions from various multinational corporations, including Ford and General Motors." By December, President Silva instituted AI-5, a bill that shuttered the National Congress, imposed strict censorship on media, and suspended habeas corpus.

"Military authorities either ignored Brazilian popular musicians or exalted them as international representatives of Brazilian culture," wrote Dunn. But as the year went on, the Tropicalistas began to garner unwanted attention from the authorities. As Veloso told Dunn: "The military didn't know what to make of it—they didn't know whether it was a political movement or not—but they saw it as anarchic and they feared it." The Tropicalistas and their irreverence were more dangerous to the regime than any protest song.

Two weeks after AI-5 went into effect, the police arrived at Veloso's home to arrest him and Gil. The two singers were imprisoned for two months, put into solitary confinement, unable to contact their friends and family. In Veloso's recollection, he verged on madness during that time—neither interrogated nor charged with any crime, instead left in a purgatorial state that he compared to a bad ayahuasca trip, uncertain if normalcy would ever return to his life.

Only near the end of their imprisonment did Veloso finally learn how they had run afoul of the dictatorship. Soon after the riot at FIC, the disqualified Veloso, Gil, and Os Mutantes played a concert in Rio under a banner also designed by Oiticica. It featured the body of slain favela gangster Cara de Cavalo, one of the first victims of the death squads, with the caption "Seja marginal, seja heroi" (Be a criminal, be a hero). In the weeks after, that performance became distorted by radio and television personality, Randal Juliano, "a demagogue in the fascist style who courted the dictatorship," as Veloso put it. Juliano embellished the details of the night to stoke the flames of outrage, saying the Tropicalistas slandered the flag and national anthem. Juliano directly asked the military to make an example of them and it complied.

Ultimately, Veloso and Gil were released without incident, but forbidden to perform in public (a far worse fate befell singer Victor Jara in Chile, who was tortured and executed, his body left in the street). Unable to play concerts—outside of one performance to raise money for their plane fare out of the country—they were exiled from Brazil and, for the next four years, resided in London. Both recorded English albums while living there, but that bright, vivacious sound of their earlier work was noticeably muted, even as they drew on English rock and a sound picked up from Caribbean immigrants, reggae.

In January 1972, no longer perceived as a threat by the military, the two were allowed to return to their homeland for good, now hailed as heroes by their fans. But much like their fellow Tropicalistas, they too had moved on from that era-defining sound. Gal Costa became the most famous of

125

the collective, while Os Mutantes' frontwoman Rita Lee struck out on a successful solo career and the remaining members of the group delved more into complicated progressive rock moves. The irascible Tom Zé continued to make itchy, prickly, idiosyncratic music, at times rendering samba rhythms out of blenders and belt sanders.

Even as the country's nationalism was at a peak (thanks to the Pelé-led national team winning their third World Cup title in 1970), it was a depressed time for artists. As torture, exile, censorship, and murder suppressed anything approaching outspokenness, the post-Tropicália years became "vazio cultural" (cultural void) or "the suffocation." And while the Tropicalistas became beloved stars in Brazil and even enjoyed acclaim in the U.S., as the impeachment of President Dilma Rousseff and near-calamitous 2016 summer olympic games make clear, the rampant corruption and great disparity between rich and poor malings the country to this day.

But the sonic example of Tropicália continued to resonate. A new generation of Brazilians sprang up immediately in their wake and made adventurous MPB, from rocker Raul Seixas to commune hippies Os Novos Baianos and the feather-boa-clad Secos & Molhados. And when David Byrne reissued a compilation of Tom Zé's music in 1990 (and Os Mutantes in 1999), he opened up a new generation of alternative and indie musicians to Brazil's sonic delights, with artists ranging from Beck to Nelly Furtado to Panda Bear all smitten by its charms. More recently, São Paulo's "samba sujo" scene garnered more notice, contributing to Elza Soares' acclaimed 2016 LP *A Mulher Do Fim Do Mundo* (*The Woman at the End of the World*)—and acts like Passo Torto, Thiago França, and Metá Metá prove that Tropicália's mutant spirit is still vital.

The art experiment enacted by these young musicians didn't conquer the dictatorship, though it provided hope and light in the country's darkest years. As Veloso noted, he and his friends strived to get out from under the shadow of the American Empire and to elevate Brazil to world prominence: "Tropicalismo wanted to project itself as the triumph over two notions: one, that the version of the Western enterprise offered by American pop and mass culture was potentially liberating... and two, the horrifying humiliation represented by capitulation to the narrow interests of dominant groups, whether at home or internationally." Almost 50 years later, the vibrant sound and indomitable spirit the Tropicalistas conjured is still on the loose. ✎

JOAN BAEZ PERFORMS AT LIVE AID BENEFIT CONCERT
PHILADELPHIA, PENNSYLVANIA, JULY 13, 1985.

"I'm tired of human lives turned into hashtags and prayer hands. We are facing ourselves as a nation, as a race of humans, we are facing our worst habits. And it's time. It is time now to make a difference. It is time now to act or change, because we all have the possibility of having and raising our very own children who can possibly die innocently."

—MIGUEL, PITCHFORK MUSIC FESTIVAL 2016